The Chaplain
of Bourbon Street

The Chaplain
of Bourbon Street

BY BOB HARRINGTON

WITH WALTER WAGNER

impact books

Nashville, Tennessee

*The people described in this book are real.
However, to protect the innocent,
the names, except for publicly known figures,
have been changed.*

For the three women I love
Joyce, Rhonda and Mitzi

CONTENTS

The Chaplain
of Bourbon Street

1

A VISIT FROM SUNBEAM

The word spread fast along Bourbon Street.

No one had invited me—a sin-busting, devil-chasing young preacher—into the hellhole that was the French Quarter of New Orleans.

In the courtyard leading to my office I hung a flaming red cross, bathed in a yellow spotlight, that could be seen clearly from the street. On the sidewalk I placed a wooden signboard that invited the lost, the damned and the troubled inside for counseling, aid, prayer and comfort.

The cross and sign were an affront to the powerful, money-hungry owners of the honky-tonk strip joints and bars that front Bourbon Street like so many open manhole covers.

I was an interloper, a stranger who had no place in an area dedicated to perverted pleasure. Preaching the Lord's word in this heartland of heathenism was no way to win friends and influence people.

I knew that my ministry on Bourbon Street was going to be difficult. I had no illusions. But Mark's injunction, ". . . Go ye into all the world, and preach the gospel to every creature," strengthened my resolve.

I had shoehorned my way in, and the next move was up to my natural enemies, the tough, no-nonsense club owners who would stop at nothing to root me out.

I half expected a bomb to be tossed through the window of my office. Threatening anonymous phone calls wouldn't have surprised me. Perhaps a fire would leave my Bible, tracts and pamphlets in smoking ruins. A hired hood might point a gun at my head and warn me to leave.

But when the challenge came, it was far more subtle and indirect.

I was to be unmasked as a real-life Elmer Gantry, and the weapon chosen for my disgrace was sex.

A modern-day Delilah was sent to do the job.

She was the most famous and beautiful stripper on the street. Her measurements—42-25-36—were legendary. Five giant pictures of her in pasties and G-string adorned the outside of the club where she worked. Inside, souvenir photos, matchbooks and cocktail napkins all displayed her amazing torso. Her "Dance of Love"—a performance in which she simulated the climactic moment of orgasm—had aroused thousands of men.

She had a soft North Carolina drawl and the face of an angel.

"My name is Sunbeam," she said, moving into a chair in my private office. She sat and crossed her legs, her skirt inching up to her thighs. Taking off her sunglasses, she shook her head. A cascade of blond hair fell to her shoulders.

"Reverend, I hope you're not too busy to see me. If you're tied up, we could talk at my apartment later tonight."

"We'll talk right here."

"They tell me you're an evangelist." She laughed and showed a perfect set of white teeth. "I'm something of an evangelist myself. I go into the world preaching sex."

"And you've probably won more converts on Bourbon Street that I ever will."

She laughed again. But this time the sound had an edge of nervousness. I wasn't shaping up as an easy conquest.

"Does your wife satisfy you?" she asked suddenly.

"In every way."

"No one would ever know if you slept with me."

"God would."

She recrossed her legs and looked directly at me.

"You're too damn good-looking a man to waste your time being a preacher."

"And you're too good-looking a woman to sell your body."

"Oh, I won't charge *you*."

"You just didn't wander in here accidentally. You're being paid by someone."

"That's not true," she said, her voice rising in anger.

I pushed my Bible toward her. "Swear to it on the Book."

She ignored the challenge.

"I can have any man I want."

"Not me."

"Don't you think I'm beautiful?"

"Jesus changed me a few years ago, but He surely didn't cut out my eyes. The Lord must have worked overtime in creating you."

The unexpected praise gave her courage.

"Don't you think my hair is beautiful?"

"Yes, it's beautiful. But it's going to burn in hell if you don't get your heart right with God."

"I don't believe in hell."

"That won't make the temperature down there one degree cooler."

"I don't believe in God."

"The Bible says, 'The fool has said in his heart there is no God.' "

"I taught Sunday School when I was sixteen, and the

deacon tried to unzip my dress. Your churches are full of hypocrites."

"You're fifty per cent right because most churches are only half filled on Sunday mornings."

"At least strippers aren't hypocrites. We are what we are. We show what we have."

"And more. But you're still one of the biggest hypocrites I've ever met."

"You're a damned fool if you believe that."

"You're a hypocrite on stage. You wear false eyelashes. You blow up your breasts with silicone. You smear on rouge and lipstick. And you pretend to enjoy taking off your clothes in front of men."

"Shut up," Sunbeam screamed as she rose to her feet and pointed her forefinger at me. "You're a good-for-nothing son-of-a-bitch."

"I'm a saved Baptist minister in the service of God."

"You're a self-righteous bastard."

"You're wrong. We're all sinners. All of our attempts at righteousness are as filthy rags in the sight of God."

Sunbeam looked at her watch, regained her composure, and sat down again.

"Can't you talk about anything except God and religion?"

"I can—but I want to show you how to surrender your life to Jesus. Even now, God's Spirit is drawing you to that decision."

Sunbeam bolted from the chair and flounced to the door. "I don't want your damned God," she shouted.

I could hear the clatter of her heels outside. I breathed easier, knowing I had passed my first test on Bourbon Street. Whoever had sent Sunbeam to compromise me had failed. I wondered what price Sunbeam would have to pay for that failure.

I heard nothing from her directly for two weeks. But I suspected she was calling me on my office telephone. It would ring every evening about 10 P.M. When I picked up the receiver, no one would answer, but each night I would hear the same strident music playing in the background before the phone would suddenly go dead.

Then, unexpectedly, Sunbeam came back to my office. This time she was dressed quietly, and there was no arrogance or sarcasm in her manner.

"Reverend," she began, "you've got to help me. I've called you every night since I walked out of here. Each time, I wanted to talk to you, but I didn't know what to say. Something is wrong with me."

"Sunbeam," I said, "I want you to spend the weekend with my family."

The girl was flabbergasted.

"But why?"

"Let's just say a change in atmosphere might help us work a miracle."

Sunbeam picked up my phone and dialed a number. She was calling her boss to tell him that she wouldn't be working that weekend. After a short conversation, Sunbeam hung up. Her face was ashen.

"He said that for missing Saturday and Sunday, the days he does his biggest business, he was going to slash my breasts with a razor blade."

Shaking, Sunbeam leaned on my arm as we walked out to my car for the drive home.

But by the time we reached my apartment, Sunbeam's mood had brightened considerably. She was determined that she was going to enjoy herself and forget about what she had to face with her disgruntled employer until Monday.

Sunbeam was effusively welcomed by my wife, Joyce, and my two teen-age daughters, Rhonda and Mitzi.

The girls immediately took her under their wing. They followed the stripper around like obedient puppies. Soon I began wondering if it had been a good idea to bring Sunbeam home. I overheard Rhonda asking Sunbeam, "How old do you have to be to become a stripper?"

In the kitchen, Joyce said to me worriedly, "From the way it's going, Bourbon Street may have the reverend's two daughters stripping in a couple of years."

I told her, "Wait. That glamour is only skin-deep. The girls will break through her veneer."

I went out to the living room and found my daughters sitting cross-legged at Sunbeam's feet. They were plying her with questions, and Sunbeam was obviously basking in the adulation.

At supper the undisguised admiration of Sunbeam continued. "Your life must be really exciting," Mitzi said.

Joyce dropped the gravy bowl, splattering the carpet. She seemed about to say something, but held back. I could tell she was exercising enormous self-control.

"What's wrong, Mother?" Rhonda asked.

"I'm just a little nervous tonight," my wife answered. She got up and bolted for the kitchen.

I wondered again if it had been a good idea to bring Sunbeam home. Had I made a mistake? I had hoped that the stripper would be inspired by my family, so inspired that she would accept Jesus, leave Bourbon Street, marry a good man and begin her own family. I never thought Rhonda and Mitzi would view her as an idol.

I joined Joyce in the kitchen.

"The way they treat her, you'd think she was the Queen of Sheba," Joyce said indignantly.

I had no answer, except to pray. Our kitchen sink became an altar. Together, Joyce and I asked God to open the eyes of our daughters, to accept Sunbeam, but to accept her as a transgressor who needed help.

I went back into the dining room in time to hear Rhonda say, "But, Sunbeam, you shouldn't damn my teacher because he gave me a bad grade in math. I deserved the mark he gave me."

"Goddamn him anyway," Sunbeam said.

"No, no, no," Rhonda shouted. "You can't damn anyone in this house."

Rhonda burst into tears. So did Sunbeam. The stripper was visibly shaken, upset that she had caused Rhonda to cry.

"I guess I can't do anything right," Sunbeam said. "What's wrong with me?"

"You need Jesus," I said.

"I can't . . . couldn't accept Him. That would mean giving up a salary of five hundred dollars a week."

"In the long run, you would be gaining more."

"No, I can't." Sunbeam looked at Rhonda and Mitzi. "I don't belong here."

Sunbeam put on her coat. "At least on Bourbon Street they accept me for what I am. Take me back."

"Christ must come into your life sooner or later. Why postpone your decision?"

"I just can't, that's all."

I drove Sunbeam back toward Bourbon Street. It was a quiet ride. I felt that the girl was struggling for inner strength, but was losing the battle. I made one last try.

"Let me stop the car and we'll pray here at the side of the road."

"I'm sorry, Reverend, it wouldn't work. No matter where I went, they'd find me, scar me for life, maybe even kill me."

Her mind was made up, and it was impossible for her to let the Lord into her life.

Sunbeam returned to stripping, the only thing she knew. But now her heart wasn't in it. In the following weeks, I visited her club, but she wouldn't see me. I called her several times, but she slammed down the phone each time she heard my voice.

Meantime, the reports I received about her weren't encouraging. She was drinking heavily and had become a lesbian.

The tragic end of Sunbeam's story came sooner than I expected. Her premonition of death, I discovered, was justified.

The barker who worked outside her club called me at three o'clock in the morning.

"They just found Sunbeam," he said, "and her gorgeous throat was cut from ear to ear."

I woke Joyce and told her the news. We prayed for Sunbeam, knowing full well the star-crossed girl had died unhappy and unsaved. They never found her killer. But I know who Sunbeam's murderer was. Bourbon Street.

2

GENESIS

I was born September 2, 1927.

I was born again April 15, 1958.

Both my births occurred in Sweet Water, Alabama, which lies in the western portion of the state near the Tombigbee River. On a map of Alabama, Sweet Water is all but invisible, a dot in the midst of the rolling clay prairies of the black belt. When I was a boy, a scant four hundred souls called it home. The "downtown" area was a dirt-road junction with three stores, a bank, a barbershop, a post office and a gas station. We didn't have a mayor or a policeman.

Logging and cotton farming were the only industries and while I was growing up (before the advent of television), fishing for perch in the local creek, bordered by sun-colored buttercups, was the town's major diversion.

I was born big, about eleven pounds. My head was enormous in proportion to the rest of my body. As a top-heavy baby, I tilted even as I took my first steps. I don't think my hat size was ever less than seven. Folks laughed when my father pulled back the blanket in my crib and showed me off. The laughter enraged my father and mother. They considered me a special blessing since my brother, born a year before, had died at birth.

The death of my parents' first-born and their gratitude for

my safe passage into the world (despite my outsized head) triggered a permissiveness in my upbringing. My brother, Jerry, came along four years later and as children we were allowed to run wild. I recall that by the age of nine I had a faculty for getting exactly what I wanted. I was allowed to swim in the creek whenever my fancy dictated, and I was often gone from home hours at a time on fishing excursions or to pick blackberries in the railroad-bar ditches outside town.

My mother, a trim, intelligent, always well-meaning woman, tried with little success to improve the cultural side of my life. I was given trumpet, violin and dancing lessons—but it was torture to practice and my attention wandered easily.

Amid grinding poverty all around me, I was fortunate to be born into a prosperous family. My parents, Robert and Ludie Harrington, were childhood sweethearts who married in 1925. My dad had come to Sweet Water years before, working first as a common laborer. He saved his money and eventually acquired three successful businesses—a sawmill, a farm that employed thirty-eight Negro families and the general store which sold everything from shoes to slop jars.

My dad was "Mr. Sweet Water," a kind and generous man who, to my knowledge, only lost his temper once.

Marengo County, in which Sweet Water is located, was dry, but there was a lot of bootlegging, and moonshine and home brew were in plentiful supply. On Saturday nights, many of the men in town would gather at my father's store and they would drink steadily as the night wore on. My father would tolerate the drinking, but put his foot down firmly when any of the men began using foul language. He didn't want anyone cursing around my mother. One Saturday night a man who was a foot taller and fifty pounds heavier than my father began using abusive language. My father grabbed him and shoved him out the door. The man came back in and hit him on the head with the blunt end of a knife. A spurt of blood that looked like Old Faithful came gushing out of his head. In a towering rage, my father grabbed his .22-caliber rifle and aimed it at the man. One shot from that gun would have changed the destiny of my family. I would have been the son of a murderer. I realized this instinctively and grabbed the gun from my father's hands. He stared at me for a full minute, breathing hard. I didn't know whether he would react with reason or passion.

"Don't kill him, don't kill him," I begged.

My father took another look at the man. Then, without saying a word, he walked out of the store.

To this day, I'm grateful to the Lord because He gave my father the strength to overcome his flash of homicidal anger. How different my life would have been if that trigger had been pulled.

I hid the gun and ran for the doctor, who came at once and treated my father's head.

The incident was never mentioned again.

Because of my father's influence, people were afraid not to grant my slightest wish—fearing their credit would be cut off at the store. I didn't realize this or knowingly take advantage of it—but somehow things always seemed easier for me than for any of the other kids in town.

I would have been totally spoiled except for the hard-handed discipline of my maternal grandmother, Mama Shoultz, a gallant lady who visited us frequently and completely dominated our household from the moment she arrived. She cooked berry cobbler pies, mopped the floors, washed the windows and, to my consternation, applied a broomstick handle to my backside when I needed it.

It was my grandmother who also introduced me to religion. There were two houses of worship in Street Water, a

Methodist church up on the hill and a Baptist church down in the valley. The churches were the focal points of the town's social life, combination civic clubs and community centers where the women had their supper meetings. They were places to go for fellowship—not necessarily to worship God. I remember how the men used to sit outside on the backs of their cars and curse and gossip while the women would go inside and sing songs and listen to the preachers.

We happened to belong to the Methodist church, but as a boy I felt no particular need for the Lord. My parents did insist that I attend Sunday School, but I complied only out of a sense of duty. I would much rather have been fishing or picking blackberries.

I had not been formally admitted to the church, a condition which outraged my grandmother, even though I was still a stripling of nine.

On a July afternoon in 1936, one day after grandma had arrived for her latest visit, I was sitting with her on the back porch of our big, rambling house.

"Bobby, there's a revival at the church this evening," she announced, "and I think we should go." Her tone was resolute, her manner determined. There was no point in making excuses or arguing.

At 7:30 P.M., shepherded by grandma, I found myself comfortably seated in the second pew of our small frame church.

The service began with a short, stocky, red-faced evangelist bellowing fire and brimstone.

"If you want to go to heaven," he thundered, "get yourself right with the Lord." He went on to quote Scripture in a loud, authoritative voice. But despite his passion and the volume of sound coming from the pulpit, I did an unforgivable thing. My eyelids grew heavier and heavier, and before long I was sound asleep.

The next thing I knew I felt a firm hand shaking me awake.

"Bobby, I want you to do something special for me," said grandma. "It will make your dad and mother very proud of you."

"What is it?"

"I want you to join the church!"

"If you say so, Grandma."

"I want you to walk down the aisle and shake hands with Brother James when the choir starts singing the second verse of 'Shall We Gather at the River?'"

"Yes, ma'am."

I got up and hit the sawdust trail. I shook the preacher's hand and he said, "God bless you."

Suddenly there was a crowd around me, and people were hugging my neck and shoulders. They were jubilant and happy. Someone shouted, "Little Bobby Harrington is saved." Saved from what? I had no idea. Grandma came up and kissed me. I had a warm feeling all over. I was glad she was so pleased.

But the experience remained a mystery to me. I felt unchanged, no different from the boy I was before the church took me into the fold. The hosannas of the congregation and the preacher's blessing wore off quickly. I felt no emotion, no pouring forth of faith. No one had mentioned giving my *heart* to Jesus. No one had mentioned I could ask Him into my heart so He could save my soul.

Joining the church did make my parents happy. There was an extra dessert when we got home and told them the news.

But my life continued to flow as always, a boy growing up

in a small town, a boy who loved mischief and had no idea in the world of the rich life that a true Christian could live.

God, if I thought about Him at all, was only a hazy, shapeless mass—far removed from the reality of my everyday life. What was real to me was the atmosphere of my father's store. The pungent smell of Blood Hound chewing tobacco, the acrid aroma of turpentine, the bins of crisp turnip greens, the flowered patterns of yard goods piled high on the counters.

And the drummers—they were real, too. I would listen by the hour as they talked about their travels. Most of the time, they complained of the hard life of a salesman on the road. They were openly envious of the success of their employers—how easy their superiors had it sitting in the home office while they trudged their wares through every backwater town in Alabama.

It amazed me that these men did little but complain about improving their stature in the world. I always found myself admiring not the drummers but their employers, because they were the men who were the earthshakers, the doers, the successful men who could afford to hire others to sell their merchandise.

The drive for success was a mesmerizing force in my life, even as a small boy. Though I didn't understand the nature of success—and wouldn't until I was thirty-one years old and reborn in the grace of God—I had a tremendous desire to excel.

In the games we played as children, I had to be the leader, though most of my playmates were four or five years older. If we played soldiers, I was always the general. I remember once during a game of soldiers, one of my friends appeared with sergeant's stripes stitched gaudily on the sleeve of his shirt. I was outraged. Not to be outdone, I went home and had my mother sew stripes on my sleeve that ran from the top of the shoulder to the bottom of my cuff.

Charles Lindbergh was my hero. His daring solo flight across the Atlantic had captured my imagination and I read everything I could find about him. I walked around with my precious Lindbergh aviator cap, complete with goggles. Finding a cap to fit my big head was impossible, so my mother bought the largest size available, cut out a piece in the back and filled it with elastic. Only then did it fit.

We had a shower and an inside bathroom installed in the house, and one memorable day I went with my parents to Demopolis to buy the ultimate luxury—a radio. It was a big, bulky thing and my father put it in the store so people could gather round and listen. The favorite program was "Lum and Abner." When he closed the store, my father would pile the radio into the car and take it home. From store to home, from home to store, that radio was rarely out of my dad's sight.

I continued to go to church and I learned all my Sunday School lessons. But I might as well have been a heathen for all the good it did me. In my heart of hearts I knew I was just going through the motions. I hadn't been saved at all. I had both feet firmly planted in hell, and, if I had died then and there, that's where I would have landed.

Though I was spiritually immature, physically I was growing up fast. My body began catching up with my head.

Meantime, I mooned my way through grade school, finding little in the curriculum to challenge me. Then, unexpectedly, that schoolhouse came alive—and it had nothing to do with reading, writing or arithmetic. There was a new girl in class and her name was Joyce Compton. She came from the tiny neighboring town of Nanafalia. I had never seen anyone so lovely—and I fell in love with her immediately and am still in love with her to this day. Joyce, a blond, oval-faced girl who loved animals, came into my life with shuddering impact.

I carried her books and we often did our homework together. I sent away to Texas, after scraping up $1.98, for a ring with her picture inserted in it, which I wore all the time. I tried my darndest to be a perfect gentleman whenever I was with Joyce, but she probably found me somewhat obnoxious, a strutting, arrogant boy who bragged and talked too much.

Soon after meeting Joyce, I confided to my mother that I had discovered the girl I was going to marry.

"Mom," I asked, "how will I know if I'm really in love?"

She shrugged and answered, "Don't worry, Son, you'll know."

When I told my mother that the girl I loved was Joyce Compton, she chuckled. I found out why a few years later— my mother and father and Joyce's folks were close friends and used to double-date before they were married. They never dreamed that one day they would have children who would grow up and marry. But that's what happened.

I had a quick mind and an agile tongue, and though I did precious little studying, I sailed through school.

As a big, lumbering boy, I easily made the high-school football team, playing center and getting my share of bruises and bone-jarring jolts in every game. We didn't have a lighted field or bleachers. People would walk up and down the side of the field to follow the action. Joyce was a cheerleader and played the drums. I was the busiest fellow on the squad. I was in action a full sixty minutes during the game and at half time I played the trumpet in the band. I was the only boy in the band wearing a football uniform.

When we won a game we'd march downtown in a victory celebration. The march would usually end at my father's store, and he'd bring out a huge carton of ice cream as a treat for us.

When I turned fourteen, the Japanese bombed Pearl Harbor, and I was sent to Marion Military Institute High School in Marion, Alabama—a preparatory step, in my dad's mind, for my entrance into West Point or Annapolis. Actually, it was a reform school with tuition. I piled up demerits fast and was frequently punished by being forced to run around the bull ring.

But thank the Lord I went to Marion. For the first time in my life, I wasn't coddled, and I learned the value of discipline. I began to study with a vengeance. I also made the football team and joined the band, this time playing violin. I carried my violin case all over the campus, and I was laughed at by the other boys. I just looked funny—a hulking, strapping boy, member of the football squad, carrying that case around everywhere. I was called sissy and chicken and the boys who laughed the loudest were the ones who couldn't play the radio without picking up static.

In shame, I sent the violin home.

It was one of the biggest mistakes I ever made. Only years later did I realize what a foolish thing that was. If anyone has the talent to play the violin, the trumpet or even a jug, do it for the Lord and don't let anybody discourage you. I hadn't learned that lesson yet.

At Marion we were forced to go to church. On Sunday mornings the Baptists and the Methodists would fall in and we would march in formation to our respective houses of worship. I would have given anything to be a Baptist, because we Methodists had to march seventeen blocks farther than the Baptists. My religious convictions became no stronger; I just wore out more shoe leather.

My only other religious activity was regular attendance at

the Baptist Training Union. I went not out of conviction but because the prettiest girls in town also attended.

I kept my grades up, but my biggest thrill at Marion was playing football. I had blossomed into my full height and weight—six feet two and 225 pounds. I was chosen all-state center for two consecutive years. I was also elected president of the student body and for the first time in my life I learned how to shoot dice, usually losing my weekly allowance shortly after it arrived from home.

For my prowess on the football field, I received scholarship offers to eight schools. I chose Auburn University. But playing football at Auburn was vastly different from Marion. In military school, I had been the tallest, heaviest boy, but at the university I was like a Chihuahua among a pack of Great Danes.

As far as church was concerned, I simply didn't go. Who felt like going to church after one of those Saturday-night fraternity parties? I didn't have my mother and father or grandma to make me go; the military wasn't there to march me; there was nobody in particular to wake me up on Sunday mornings.

Instead, I picked up a couple of obnoxious habits.

While I was being rushed by one of the fraternities, one of the boys said, "Bob, you don't smoke, do you?"

I told him, "No. The coach told me not to."

He said, "Then how are you going to fit in with the group?"

I asked if I had to smoke to fit in with the group.

My fraternal overseer answered with a resounding, "Yes."

"All right," I said, "let me have a cigarette."

I choked on the first puff and didn't inhale. I thought I was going to be sick—but I gradually acclimated myself to the new experience of smoking.

One night I was riding in a car with a group of my fraternity pals. The fellow next to me said, "Bob, you don't drink, do you?"

I told him I didn't. "The coach said I wasn't to drink anything stronger than Coca Cola."

He said, "One or two beers won't hurt you."

"If I have to, I will," I said.

That was back when you had to work hard to get a beer can open. They didn't have zippers on them. You had to have a screwdriver, a nail or a church key.

I never will forget my first taste of beer. It was awful. I pretended to swallow some, but everytime we passed a dark place I would spit it out onto the road. In that way I set a new beer consumption record for the fraternity—ten cans.

Smoking and drinking added to the tough image I was supposed to have as a swinging college boy. Deep down, I didn't really think I was tough, but it was easier to go along with the crowd I was running with than to protest. I hadn't yet developed the inner security that comes with embracing the Lord.

One day we had an intra-squad game, a game that was to end my football career at Auburn. I'd always resented the fact that all the glory went to the backs on the team and the linemen took their punishment in anonymous agony. On this particular day, there was a cameraman from the local paper taking pictures and I thought if only I could block a punt the camera might catch my heroic action and I would be IT that night at the fraternity party.

I found a little daylight between guard and tackle. I went racing through as the opposing player started to punt. I closed my eyes, jumped up—but I missed the man. Instead, I went sailing directly into a steel goal post. When I woke up the next day, I called my dad and said, "I want to join the Navy." At first, he was disillusioned because I wasn't ready to wait for an appointment to one of the military academies, but he masked his disappointment and said, "Son, that's mighty patriotic of you."

It wasn't patriotism at all. I was scared. I knew I could get killed out on that football field.

My parents signed the papers for their brave he-man, and soon I found myself fighting the battle of the Great Lakes Naval Training Station in Illinois.

Almost the first thing I was confronted with was a General Classification Test. I filled in my name and address, but when it came to the space marked "religion" I was confused. There were three choices: Catholic, Jew or Protestant. I knew I wasn't a Catholic, I didn't even know how to pronounce it. I doubted strongly that I was Jewish. I punched the boy next to me and said, "I'm hung up on this religion bit here. Would you mind helping me?"

He said, "I'm a Catholic myself."

He asked me what church I belonged to. I told him I had attended the Methodist church back home.

"Then," he said, "you're a Protestant. Put that down."

I checked Protestant, figuring the Navy only wanted to know my religion so they could bury me in the proper cemetery in case I expired in the line of duty.

That was all the allusion there was to religion. I was thrown in with Baptists, Jews, Catholics and other Methodists. But nobody ever talked to me about the Lord. Nobody asked me if I was saved. Nobody ever talked to me about my soul. Wouldn't it be wonderful if our young men, upon entering the service, were asked if they would live for Jesus during their military tour? I'm sure there were devout believers among my buddies in service, but I never met any.

I took courses in seamanship and did endless marching around the base. On Sundays I was too tired and too disinterested to go to church. I continued to gamble, smoke, drink, and on liberty I chased as many girls as anybody else from our boot camp.

The Japanese had surrendered while I was in training— so I was discharged within a year. There was nothing gallant about my service in the Navy; I was only thankful that it was such a short tour. Inside myself, I was deeply dissatisfied, but I didn't know what was causing the emotional feeling of self-hatred that I had developed.

I was sent to New Orleans for discharge. My folks came to meet the boy they had sent off to service. My mother hugged and kissed me. Tears rolled down my father's cheeks. But they didn't realize that I had changed completely. I came home with habits in my life that I was ashamed of. My heart had grown cold and hard. My love for my parents wasn't there. My love for my brother wasn't there. I was a different person. It wasn't the Navy's fault—it was no one's fault but my own.

The first night I met my folks in New Orleans proved that I had changed. Instead of sitting down and telling them about my experiences at Great Lakes, I parked them at a hotel and left for a tour of the French Quarter with an old girl friend who happened to be in town. I spent practically all my mustering-out pay visiting the dives and strip joints of the Quarter and when I returned to the hotel my parents were asleep.

After the formalities of my discharge were completed, my folks took me home to Sweet Water.

I was lost, confused and filled with doubt and self-loathing.

3

A DOOR OPENS

I decided to accept a football scholarship to the University of Alabama—I was hoping their goal post might be a little softer.

My mother had always wanted me to be a doctor, so I enrolled as a pre-med student. Before long I could name every joint in the body and every joint in town. Saturday nights I made the rounds of the local beer halls with my fraternity pals. The rest of the week, when I wasn't playing or practicing for a game, I studied hard.

Pricked by my own guilt, one day in anatomy class I asked the professor, "You've explained how muscles work, you've told us about the vascular and nervous systems, but where is the conscience located in the human body?"

"It's in there someplace, young man," the professor replied, a hint of annoyance in his voice.

I persisted. "But where?" A wave of laughter rippled through the room, and the professor was now becoming decidedly uneasy.

"I said it was inside you somewhere, but medical science can't draw you a precise diagram. The location of the conscience is a spiritual matter."

I was dissatisfied with the explanation, and added, "Wouldn't it be wonderful if we could find some way to cut out a man's guilty conscience? We could charge five hundred dollars for the operation and call it a 'guilty conscience-ectomy.'"

The class broke out in another round of laughter. Then the bell rang and the lecture was over. That professor never did give me a satisfactory answer. I hadn't asked the question facetiously—but out of a deep need of my own. I was still full of doubts, fears and uncertainties. It didn't occur to me to talk over my problems with a clergyman and I wasn't interested in taking a course in theology.

Time passed swiftly and in my junior year I decided to start a photography business on campus. Friday and Saturday were my big nights—the doors to the frat houses were thrown wide open for dances and parties. Liquor flowed freely and many of the couples, freed from the week-long grind of study and discipline, joyously insisted on posing in lewd positions. Sunday morning I always had a flock of calls, now-sober coeds begging me to destroy the negatives and boys offering to pay me not to develop and print the pictures. I always honored these requests.

Soon my photography sideline became a booming business. Money was really rolling in.

All through college I had kept in touch with Joyce, writing and telephoning her frequently. We made plans for her to study at Alabama, too. When she arrived on campus she was still the loveliest thing I had ever seen—a serious, down-to-earth, God-fearing Baptist girl who somehow reciprocated the deep love I had for her.

I proposed immediately. I was surprised when she accepted, and before she could change her mind I hurried her off to a parsonage for the wedding. We were married in the sight of God—but the religious references the minister made to "holy matrimony" rolled over me without effect.

After our honeymoon, Joyce talked to me about religion. There it was again, always with me, tempting me, baiting me, hanging around like an unwanted relative who has moved permanently into your home.

"Are you going to become a Baptist?" Joyce asked.

"Not on your life. Those Baptists don't believe in anything. Besides, they're too narrow."

"Then," Joyce responded with conviction, "I'll become what you are—a Methodist."

So the next Sunday we went to the Trinity Methodist Church. At the end of the service the pastor issued an invitation for non-members to join the congregation. Joyce jabbed me in the side and said, "Come on, let's go." I thought I was back with grandma.

We got up and a steward guided us to the first pew. Smelling of nicotine, he handed us a card. "Fill this out," he said. The card asked for a profession of faith. I didn't know what that meant. I felt confused, and it reminded me of the form I had filled out in the Navy. I told the steward, "Look, all I want to do is join."

He said, "Then just fill in your name and address."

I did. Now I was a member, presumably in good standing, of the Trinity Methodist Church.

Soon I was appointed president of the Young Adult Sunday School Class; then I became a junior steward. At Christmas time I even took part in the church pageant. I played a wise man. There I was on stage with a blanket wrapped around me, holding a crooked stick and standing knee-deep in hay (to which I was allergic—it was a miracle that I didn't sneeze through the entire re-enactment of the birth of Christ). I felt silly and out of place. But after the play was over people told me I was excellent as a wise man. Actually, I was the dumbest man in the congregation. Standing there as lost as I could be. But that's religion for most people. That's what goes on in churches all around the country—people playing at being Christians. They draw you in and say, "Fill out this card. If you can't fill it out, we'll do it for you. If you can't come back, just mail your tithe. If you can't mail it, we'll come and pick it up. And call us when you need a good funeral."

Joyce and I moved into a house off campus. You couldn't call it a home. I loved my wife, I was sure of that. But though we hadn't been married long, I already felt there was something crucial missing in our relationship. Rhonda, our first daughter, was born. Then Mitzi. Even with the arrival of our children, our house seemed to be suffering from an unnamed curse. Preoccupied with school and my business, I left the raising of our daughters entirely to Joyce. I didn't have the time to take a responsible part in their upbringing.

We continued to attend church on Sunday mornings. One day after services, the pastor sent some men by our house to get me to pledge, to commit myself to a certain amount of money each month. I said, "I can't make a commitment like that." I spread my hands. "Take a look around. I'm already committed, committed to the car, committed to the house, committed to the refrigerator, committed to the carpet, committed to my wife and children." Lord, I was committed to everything except the ultimate, fulfilling commitment—dedication of my life to Jesus.

The pastor's representatives went away dour-faced and empty-handed. I didn't care. I had other things to worry about. By now, I had made another crucial decision. I had decided I wasn't going to become a doctor. I didn't have the necessary drive or discipline.

I half thought of becoming a professional football player, but, since no offers from a pro team were forthcoming, I soon abandoned that idea. After finishing college, I wondered what I was going to do with the rest of my life.

For the moment, I had no choice but to continue in the photography business. I was smoking three packs of cigarettes a day, drinking heavily, and seeing other women. If Joyce suspected anything, she never let me know it. She went along with me—God knows why—as I continued my losing battle to find myself. I was, though I didn't realize it, my own worst enemy.

I think the only reason Joyce stayed with me was because there had never been a divorce in either of our families. Or perhaps it was because of Rhonda and Mitzi. She had every reason in the world to leave me—but she didn't. Nevertheless, our home was ready to cave in.

I thought a change of scene, a fresh start in a new place, might help. I closed my photography business and told Joyce that we were moving to Mobile, an Alabama community then in the throes of an insurance boom. I had decided that I wanted to sell insurance. Joyce, uncomplainingly, went along with my sudden decision. Bag, baggage and children, we drove to Mobile and found a house in the suburb of Chickasaw.

I got a job with the Liberty National Life Insurance Company, and my spirits began to perk up. I loved selling, and still do, though these days I'm selling "life assurance" rather than life insurance.

Joyce and I joined every social and fraternal organization in town. We also joined the local church. Outwardly we were considered an "ideal couple." People said Bob Harrington was going to amount to something in the community. But my relationship with Joyce was still far from ideal, still deteriorating. It had never dawned on me that when we moved to Chickasaw we would take our problems with us.

My insurance sales and commissions began to soar—and soon I broke every selling record previously established in the company. I was the leading agent in my district. Many of my prospects were picked up in nightclubs, which I visited several evenings a week. Joyce, of course, was never along.

One particular visit to a nightclub was especially memorable. Eddie Martin, the great Southern Baptist evangelist, had been holding a crusade in Mobile attended by more than fourteen thousand people. I was in the audience as the club's comedian ab-libbed a welcome to a freshly arrived group of sober-appearing citizens. The comedian said, "It's certainly nice to have you people from the Eddie Martin Crusade. Welcome to what he has been warning you about. Each of you sit down with your clean conscience and let's all go to hell together." I was among those who laughed the loudest. I never dreamed that in a few years I myself would become a member of the Eddie Martin Team. If anyone had suggested that to me, I would have called him a maniac.

After two years in the insurance business in Mobile, I began getting restless again. Although I was still racking up record-breaking sales, my boss was unnerving me, primarily because he was a religious fanatic.

During staff meetings on Friday mornings, he would bring a Baptist preacher or a religious layman in to talk to us. It was the first time I had heard of an employer forcing religion down the throats of hard-headed businessmen whose sole purpose was to sell insurance—not to listen to so-called inspirational talks about God.

After suffering through one of those weekly sermons, I approached my boss and told him, "A sales meeting is no place for religion. We only want to talk about how we can sell more insurance."

"What about the spiritual side of your life?" he asked.
I stared at him blankly. All I could manage to say was that
my wife and I attended church every Sunday.

"That's not enough," he declared. "Tell me the truth, Bob.
I know you spend many of your evenings at nightclubs when
you should be home with your wife and family. Why do you
do it?"

"I'm looking for prospects, that's why. If you want to get
the business of the hogs, you have to go where the hogs hang
out. You've got to get in and wallow with them if you want
to wallow out with their signatures on the dotted line."

"I've never asked a man to demean himself in order to
write a policy. You can find just as many prospects in places
other than nightclubs."

It was pointless to argue with him. Besides, I knew he was
right. I was only trying to justify my own reprehensible behavior.

But I didn't want to work any longer for a man who was
consumed by religion. It was ironic, I thought, that religion
dogged me every place I went despite my frantic attempts to
have as little to do with it as possible.

I also thought I was ripe for bigger things. I felt I had
enough knowledge of insurance to buy and sell the world.
And I was ready to take out my broker's license with a big
company. In any event, I wouldn't miss my employer, who
seemed to be constantly hung up on the subject of religion.

I read an ad asking for a qualified broker for the Pan
American Life Insurance Company. I went down immediately and applied for the job. I was introduced to the company's director, Jess Murray.

He greeted me warmly and listened patiently while I told
him about my record-setting sales. I was doing my best to
impress him with my prowess as an insurance agent.

After hearing me out, he leaned forward in his chair, and said, "Son, the Lord must have led you here."

"No, sir," I replied, at once suspicious that I had another religious nut on my hands. "I came down here in my car and it's parked in your lot."

"You don't understand, Mr. Harrington," he continued. "I've been praying that God would lead someone into my life and business with your personality, appearance and ability."

I was ready to walk out of his office right then. But something kept me riveted to that chair. Mr. Murray smiled and asked me to talk about my personal life.

Suddenly, I found myself pouring my heart out. I told him about my wretched existence with my family. I confided that despite my success I was deeply in debt and living beyond my means. I said I knew I was wasting my life.

"Frankly, Mr. Murray," I went on, the words coming out in a torrent, "I'm ready to go to the mat for the full count. Because of me, my home life is hell. My wife's heart is broken. Even my children know something is very wrong with their father."

Then I realized I was talking to this man like a child—yet I was already an established and successful businessman.

I paused, then broached the all-important question. "Do you want to hire me or not?"

He said, "Yes, I do."

I signed on right away.

Two days later, we had Mr. Murray to the house for dinner. As he was leaving, I went to the hall to get his coat. In the living room I could see him talking intently to Joyce.

After he left, Joyce asked me, "Do you know what Mr. Murray told me?" Without waiting for an answer, she added, "He said you needed the Lord as your Savior."

"Didn't you tell him that I'm a member of the church, an officer of the men's club, a senior steward and that I was chairman of last Saturday night's spaghetti dinner?"

"He didn't ask about all that. He just said you needed the Lord."

I shrugged, walked to the bar and poured myself a drink.

The next evening, we invited Mr. Murray and his wife to dinner at one of the finest restaurants in town.

The waitress recognized me and asked, "Your usual scotch and water, Mr. Harrington?"

"I guess so," I answered. "Anyone else care for a drink?" Joyce and the Murrays refused.

After the meal was over, I pulled out my pack of cigarettes. Nothing like a smoke to kill the taste of good food. I offered everyone at the table a cigarette. They all declined.

"Joyce," I said, "have you suddenly given up smoking?"

She was wearing spiked heels and I can still feel the point of her left shoe where she kicked me in the ankle.

"Bob," Mr. Murray said, "I used to be just like you until I got saved."

My mind flashed back to the night in Sweet Water when I had joined the church. But what good had it done me? I didn't want to pursue the conversation further. To Joyce I said, "Come on, let's dance."

The next day, Mr. Murray assigned me to open a branch office at Butler, Alabama, located just across the river from Sweet Water. Butler was a small town—but a new paper mill was moving in. That meant fresh money, loose money and loose women. The transfer also meant that I would be 110 miles away from Joyce.

The arrangement suited me fine. I worked in the daytime, visited the joints at night, then went to my parents' house to sleep. Some weekends I would go home to Joyce and the family. But she really didn't care if I came home or not. All I had to do was send the check every week.

Butler proved to be a thriving community and I was selling insurance almost as fast as I could write it. Soon I had reached the dream of every insurance man—I had sold over a million dollars worth of policies, which entitled me to join the exclusive "Million Dollar Club."

I should have been happy and pleased with myself. But I wasn't. I was thirty years old and I still didn't have a feeling of inner contentment. While visiting my parents on the night of April 15, 1958, I silently took stock of my life. There was my failing marriage, my personal unhappiness, a lack of serenity in my soul.

To drown out my negative thoughts, I tuned in my favorite television program, "Sergeant Bilko." I was soon caught up in the story—but then something made me get up and turn the set off.

"Mother," I said, "I understand there's a revival tonight at the Baptist church. I think I'll go."

She was surprised. "That's fine, Son." She could have added that I needed to get closer to the Lord, but she didn't. My mother was aware of all my personal troubles and she had a devout faith in the ability of God to solve problems.

What I didn't tell my mother was that I was going to the revival because there would be at least five good insurance prospects there, and seeing me in church would create a fine impression the next day when I called on them.

I arrived at the service late. The choir was singing a soft hymn. The church door squeaked as I opened it. I was glad. That squeaking door caused everyone to turn their heads and look at me.

A mumble went through the crowd as I walked down the aisle and found a seat in the seventh pew. Behind me I overheard two women talking. "It's Bob Harrington. Imagine!" Her companion answered, "I haven't seen him in years. I understand he's making it big as an insurance executive but his marriage is practically in the divorce court." My ears burned.

I found myself seated next to Otis, the town barber. I remembered that, when I was a child, every time Otis cut my hair he would give me a lollipop. I was really home. Otis nudged me and said, "Glad you could make it, Bob." I winked at him.

Seated near the pulpit was a visiting evangelist from Georgia, Reverend Paul Williamson. I made a mental note that he was good for at least $10,000 worth of life insurance. With all the traveling he did, it made sense for him to have a policy. I'd talk about it with him the next day.

The pastor, Reverend Jack House, was at the end of his sermon. He concluded with a pitiful plea for a love offering. I was certainly touched. When they passed the plate, I gave fifty cents. (I thought to myself, that's two packs of cigarettes —but I would make up for it easily with all the insurance I was going to sell as a result of tonight's diplomatic appearance.)

After the collection was completed, the evangelist strode into the pulpit like a conquering general. He was fiery and articulate and had the longest index finger I ever saw. Flailing his hands, he punctuated his sermon by throwing out that finger and pointing. Every time he pointed, it seemed to be straight at me.

"A lot of good people in here tonight," he declared, "are going to die and go to hell."

I didn't believe him—if people were good and lived Christian lives, why should they go to hell when they died?

The evangelist talked for forty-five minutes. He obviously

believed every word he was saying. But to me his sermon was only a long harangue. To help pass the time, I took out my prospect book and made some notes.

Finally, he was finished. I put my prospect book back into my pocket. "I claim everyone here tonight for Christ," Reverend Williamson said, issuing an invitation for all of us to come forward and be saved.

A member of the congregaton led us in a fine old hymn, "Just As I Am." I picked up my song book and started singing in a low voice. I didn't want to attract attention. As the first verse ended, I put my song book down. But the evangelist had no intention of stopping there. He said we were going to sing "Just As I Am" straight through to the fifth verse. I was surprised, I didn't know any hymn had five verses. I began to feel trapped and I was anxious to get out of there. I would have given anything for a cigarette.

On through the second, third and fourth verses we went. Then came the fifth verse:

> *Just as I am, thou wilt receive,*
> *Wilt welcome, pardon, cleanse, relieve;*
> *Because Thy promise I believe,*
> *O Lamb of God, I come! I come!*

Suddenly, my song book was getting heavier and heavier. Something was happening to me, a secret trigger was being activated. I forgot about my insurance prospects and it seemed that I was the only person in the church. My life darted hastily before my eyes—wasted talents, ability prostituted, everything noble, grand and beautiful inside me assassinated. I saw myself for what I truly was—a phony husband and father and a phony Christian.

But I was perplexed. Though I had heard that the Holy Spirit, once it had broken down your old image of yourself, could work miracles, I didn't know what to do. I didn't know you could just come to the Lord. I didn't know you could just ask His forgiveness. I didn't know you could just ask Him into your heart.

Now there was a real struggle raging within me. I was fighting God, and my immortal soul was the prize.

Then the evangelist asked us to sing the fifth verse again. I raised my voice a little louder this time. All at once, the words of that verse had tremendous meaning.

O Lamb of God, I come! I come!

I found myself in the aisle, heading up to the pulpit, knocking off a lady's hat on the way. I bumped into several pews—then I was at the altar. I had finally yielded to what was in my heart.

The evangelist stuck out his hand. I didn't want to shake hands. I grabbed him around the neck and began hugging him. The pastor came over, and I hugged him, too. Now tears were streaming down my face.

It was the most dramatic conversion in the history of the Sweet Water Baptist Church—and I was the one being converted. I could scarcely believe it.

The pastor and the evangelist took me to a little room upstairs. We all got down on our knees and prayed. They told me I was having a firsthand encounter with the Lord and that I was being saved. I kept repeating over and over again, "That's right, that's right, I'm being saved." Tears were still running down my face, the sweetest, most joyous tears I'd ever shed.

On impulse, I took out a twenty-dollar bill—all the money I had with me—and gave it to the pastor. "Split it between you," I said. I would have given $20,000 if I'd had it.

Finally, my emotion spent and my body drained of strength, I said one last prayer.

Then the pastor told me to go home.

I walked out of the church knowing I was a changed man. I wasn't sure how the experience of finding God would affect my everyday life. But now, for the first time in my life, I had a deep inner feeling of satisfaction. One of the few lines of Scripture that I knew came to mind—"Behold, I have set before thee an open door, and no man can shut it."

I drove home in a trance, bounded into the house and found my mother in the living room.

"I just got saved," I told her excitedly.

"That's real good, Bobby," she answered matter-of-factly.

"But, Mother, Mother, I've just been forgiven for all my sins. Don't you understand?"

"Have those Baptists been bothering you again, Bobby? You've been a good boy all your life. Besides, you've been a member of the church since you were nine. Don't you remember when grandma—"

"But tonight was different. I'm a new man, a new son, a new husband and a new father. Tonight I really became a Christian."

In spite of everything I said, my mother couldn't rejoice with me. She was a religious woman—but she had never been saved. She didn't realize the depth of the experience that had overtaken me.

Exhausted, I went to bed. I slept somewhere between the floor and heaven. The sheets felt like the gentle wings of angels. I even dreamed of heaven and God that night.

When I awoke the next morning, I automatically reached for my cigarettes. But I felt so good, so clean inside, that somehow I couldn't light up. I thought to myself that if the Lord Jesus Christ in the form of the Holy Spirit had come into my life last night—and the evangelist had said that my body was now the Temple of God—would it glorify the Almighty to continue the harmful habit of smoking? The answer came to me and I took the pack and tossed it into a wastebasket. I have never smoked again.

I drove to the office and soon discovered that my experience at church the night before had preceded me. Before the day was out, I was to realize that the word had spread throughout Butler and Sweet Water.

I had forgotten that I had planned a beer party that night for a group of potential clients. By now I had also made up my mind that I had taken my last drink and I wondered what I was going to tell my guests. I decided to have my secretary call and cancel the party.

I parked my car and stepped outside. A lawyer I knew, who had his office in the the same building I did, threw open his window and called down, "Bob, I hear you got religion last night."

"That's right. Do you want me to come up and tell you about it?"

"I appreciate your interest, but I'm tied up right now."

"That's the way I was. All tied up inside. But now I've found real freedom."

"It really took with you, didn't it?"

"Bone and marrow, heart and soul."

"Sometime you'll have to tell me about it. In the meantime it's more booze and women for me."

He slammed his window down and drew the shutters.

I walked to the drugstore, which was a gathering place for many of the professional men in town. As soon as I entered, a short, stocky acquaintance of mine named Herman came over. "Already heard, Bob."

"What do you think of my being saved?"

"One of the best deals you ever pulled."

"What do you mean?"

"You keep on with this kick," said Herman, "and I'll tell you what we can do. We'll get a tent and some bottles. We'll fill them full of colored liquid, put about seventy per cent alcohol in them, and you'll go around promising to heal folks and I'll sell the stuff for a dollar a bottle. We ought to make a million and we'll split it right down the middle."

"Herman, you must be joking."

"Aren't you, Bob?"

"No, I'm truly saved, and may God have mercy on your wicked soul."

I didn't know then that anybody who isn't saved thinks that people who have been saved are phonies. I thought everyone would celebrate with me. But so far no one had.

I couldn't stand the thought of selling insurance that day. It was only Wednesday, but I decided to go home to Joyce and the children and tell them about the sudden, astonishing change in my life.

Tooling along the road toward home, my head was filled only with thoughts of how surprised Joyce was going to be. She would never expect me in the middle of the week and I had already phoned her a few days before to say that I wasn't coming home for the weekend. But I knew she would be overcome with joy when she heard that the Lord had finally come into my heart.

Halfway to Chickasaw, I suddenly heard the scream of a siren behind me. I pulled over to the shoulder of the road. A highway patrol car roared up beside me and an angry officer came storming over.

"I've been chasing you for miles," he said sternly. "You were doing at least ninety."

"I guess you're right, Officer," I told him. "But I'm very

anxious to get home. I have to tell my wife that I got saved last night."

"You got what last night?"

"I got saved last night," I repeated.

"Now let me have that again. That's really a new one. Never heard that excuse before."

"Saved, s-a-v-e-d. Put it down in your book just like that."

He shook his head and stared at me. Then he wrote out my ticket.

It was beginning to rain, so I invited him into my car. "Now tell me about how you were saved," he said.

"Last night I found something I've been looking for all my life. If someone had only told me how to be saved, I would have been rescued from a life of sin twenty years ago. I didn't know how easy it was to be saved. It's the most wonderful thing that's ever happened to me."

Thoughtfully, he said, "You know, I need what you're talking about."

"It's not hard to find."

"How do you go about it?"

"Ride over to Sweet Water and listen to the evangelist. He'll show you the way."

I didn't realize that I could have led him to the Lord right there in the car. I could have prayed with him at that moment. I wasn't aware then that God wasn't particular about the atmosphere in which you saved a fellow man. The important thing was to see that he was saved. I told him go to the Sweet Water Baptist Church because I thought he had to go back to the same barn and be kicked by the same mule. The same bolt of lightning had to strike him.

But, I learned soon that lightning did strike twice in the same place. After he tore up my ticket (being saved was already beginning to pay off!), we exchanged names and addresses. Later he wrote me that he, too, had been led to the Lord.

When I arrived home, I parked in our garage and went into the house through the back door. Joyce was working in the kitchen and before she could say a word I told her, "Honey, something wonderful has happened."

Joyce arched a curious eyebrow.

"I found the Lord last night!"

"I didn't know you were looking for Him."

I deserved her skepticism. She had all the right in the world to say that, because I had previously shown no "symptoms" of becoming a Christian.

"Come here and look at me. I've already given up smoking and drinking. And that's just the beginning. From now on, a lot of other things are going to change."

"Are you being honest with me, Bob?"

"Yes, I'm being honest. I'm really saved, I'm saved."

I took her up in my arms and swung her around. Joyce began to laugh—and for the first time she believed me. She realized I was serious about my new commitment. She squeezed me hard, then began crying. Her prodigal had come home.

Joyce and I kneeled beside our kitchen table and prayed, rededicating ourselves to God and each other.

Then, arm in arm, we walked into our daughters' room. First we woke Rhonda. As she wiped the sleep from her eyes, I said, "Will you forgive me for not being a good daddy?"

That six-year-old angel said, "Oh, you haven't been a bad daddy. In fact, you're the best daddy in the whole world."

Now tears filled my eyes. I realized how much I had to make up to my family.

The noise in the room had awakened four-year-old Mitzi. "What's wrong, Daddy, what's wrong?"

I asked her the same question. "Will you forgive me for not being a good daddy?"

"I forgive you," she said with a beaming face.

If I had just come home after shooting everyone in the neighborhood, I'm sure at that moment my daughters would have forgiven me.

After we put the girls back to sleep, I asked Joyce, "Will you forgive me, too? If you will, you'll never have to worry about me again as long as we live."

"You're my husband. I love you," she answered.

For the first time, I realized how beautiful my relationship could be with my wife, how wonderful a home could be. I didn't know marriage and children were so precious until I fell in love with Jesus.

The next day, the pastor from Sweet Water called and said, "Bob, would you come up here Friday night and give your testimony?"

"Give my what?"

"Your testimony."

"I don't know what that is."

"I just want you to tell people what happened to you."

"All right," I said, "I'll be happy to do that."

On the ride back to Sweet Water, I began having the first doubts about my conversion. My family and all my old friends would be in the church to hear me. They somehow would see through me and denounce me as a sham and a fake. Worse, they might all just burst out laughing. But I gritted my teeth and decided I was going to go through with it. For thirty years I had played the devil's game, and all that Satan had done was deceive me and lie to me and almost break up my home. He had separated me from my family and nearly destroyed my life. I vowed that the devil would never again hold sway over me.

The church was jammed as I sat in my pew and waited nervously for the pastor to call me to the pulpit. When his call finally came I was scared to death. The longest speech I had ever made was five minutes and I was frightened four minutes and sixty seconds.

As I faced the congregation, I could see smiles, and on the faces of many in the crowd there was barely concealed skepticism. I opened my mouth to speak, but nothing came out. Thinking fast, I turned to our organist and asked her to play "Amazing Grace, How Sweet the Sound."

When I heard the tones of that comforting hymn, the spirit of God moved into my soul and loosened my tongue. I started talking, candidly telling of my life before Christ and how He had made me whole again. I said that if it could happen to me, it could happen to anyone. I said that Jesus had come into my heart, that my sins had been forgiven and my house had been made a home. I told them I was going to miss hell and make it to heaven.

I don't know how long I talked—but then I remembered the pastor had asked me to conclude my testimony by giving an invitation. I didn't know how to call people to the Lord, so I just said, "Ladies and gentlemen, if you want what happened to me to happen to you, too, just come forward. Christ will save you."

I paused and there wasn't a sound in the church. I've failed, I thought. Nobody believes me. Nobody is going to step forward. I couldn't get through to them, couldn't reach them, though I had never been more sincere in my life.

Then there was a stir at the back. Amazed, I saw my mother walking down the aisle. She reached me, put her hand in mine, and said simply, "Son, I want to be saved." And God saved her right there at that moment.

What a triumph, I thought. The first person I had a hand in saving was my mother. The Lord was mighty and His power without limit.

Then a man who worked in my father's store came forward. Behind him came my aunt Mittie, and before the service was over there were sixteen people at the altar, all giving their hearts to Jesus.

And it was right then, as I saw those sixteen people converted, that a new realization came to me.

I knew with certainty that the Lord had called me to preach!

He, in His mysterious way, had been preparing and testing me. Now the loud clear call was there. From now on, I wanted to spread the gospel everywhere and to everyone.

The realization was so overwhelming that I couldn't say a word. Only years later did I read a passage in Luke about the priest Zacharias that expressed my silent emotion when I knew that I was going to spend the rest of my life in the service of the Lord: "And when he came out, he could not speak unto them: and they perceived that he had seen a vision in the temple: for he beckoned unto them, and remained speechless."

4

HITTING THE SAWDUST TRAIL

Three days after my conversion, I began preaching in earnest. I gave my testimony again at the Sweet Water Baptist Church and another miracle happened.

My father, at the age of fifty-eight, came forward and dedicated his life to Christ. Dad had seen the wonders wrought in my mother and myself in the brief time since the Lord had come into our lives. My mother had a new zest for living—she had more understanding of my father's shortcomings and she went out of her way to help people less fortunate than herself. For my part, I was glorying in my new-found relationship with the Lord.

After dedicating his life to Christ, Dad also heard the call to spread the gospel, and several years later he became a licensed Methodist preacher serving a three-district circuit in Alabama.

When I told Joyce that I was leaving the insurance business to become an evangelist, she panicked. She, of course, wanted me to get religion, but she never expected I would be engulfed by it.

I couldn't blame her—I didn't have much going for me as a preacher. The Book of Job I called job; I couldn't pronounce

Deuteronomy; and I thought it was the Book of Palms instead of the Book of Psalms.

My wife was so upset that she went home for a quick visit to her mother. "Bob's gone crazy," she announced. "He wants to be a preacher and quit his job. We've got two children—how are we going to feed them?"

Joyce and her mother came to see me. I saw the commiserating look on my mother-in-law's face. "Joyce and I think you need help," she told me.

I raised my eyes heavenward. "I'm getting all the help I need."

"We're talking about a different kind of help—from a doctor."

Joyce pleaded with me, so I agreed to visit the doctor. They had already made an appointment for the next day.

What they hadn't told me was that the doctor was a psychiatrist!

I walked into his office, didn't see a couch, so I sat down in a chair behind his desk.

"How are you, Mr. Harrington?" he asked.

"I'm saved."

He nodded, looking at me doubtfully.

"What's your address? I need it for my records."

"Which one? My heavenly home or my earthly home?"

"You'd better give me the one down here." I gave him the address; then he asked, "Where were you born?"

"Which time?"

"You mean you've been born more than once?"

"Yes. I've been born twice."

"How many times do you expect to die?"

"Once. When you've been born twice, you only die once. But when you're born only once, you die twice."

"You do need help, Mr. Harrington," he said in dead earnest.

Then for forty-five minutes we talked. I explained to him how Christ had come into my life and changed me. Now I simply wanted to go into the world and preach, hoping to change the lives of others. I remembered a verse from the Bible that I had memorized the night before. "Therefore if any man be in Christ, he is a new creature. Old things are passed away; all things are become new."

After he heard me out I thought he was ready to diagnose me as a schizophrenic. Instead, he got up, snapped his brief case shut, came around to my side of the desk and dropped to his knees.

"Mr. Harrington, would you save me?"

I got down on my knees beside him, said a prayer and delivered him to the Lord.

After that, Joyce and her mother never mentioned psychiatry again.

My own mother also thought I had charted an impractical course. Two weeks after I was saved she went to see a friend of the family, Reverend Ed Folsom, who for eighteen years had untiringly preached to uncounted thousands of men and women in Alabama's prisons.

"Ed, I want you to talk to Bob," she said. "He's not working. He's quit selling insurance. All he does is preach, running around like a house afire. Remember, he's got a family to house, clothe and feed and he hasn't earned a dime since he got the call."

Ed came to see me and reported the conversation with my mother. He said, "The Lord wants you to make a living and there's nothing wrong with selling insurance."

"I can't sell insurance any more," I told him. "I talk to a man about life insurance and all I can think about is that he's going to die and I want to talk to him about Jesus."

"You've got to live."

"I'll live by preaching. Or maybe I'll starve. But that's the was it's got to be."

During the Apostle Paul's early days as a Christian, he had trouble convincing others that his testimony was sincere. ("But they were all afraid of him, and believed not that he was a disciple.")

I found myself in a similar situation. How could I convince all the people who knew me that I was completely serious in my resolve to spread the word of the Lord, that by giving up the insurance business I'd be preparing people not for death but for everlasting life.

I continued to tell everyone I met what had happened to me. I talked to Sunday School classes, on street corners, in small churches and I witnessed to my friends. Ed Folsom put me on his radio program to describe my conversion. I was only supposed to talk for five minutes, but I knew that Ed had an enormous listening audience and I wasn't about to let an opportunity like that slip away. I talked for a solid uninterrupted thirty-five minutes. Hundreds of phone calls and letters poured in after the program, most of them asking for a transcript of my testimony.

Ed took me in hand and began guiding me. "I've been trying to fire up some of these dead preachers for twenty years," he said, "and now that I've found you I'm not about to let you go."

I went with Ed into dozens of Alabama prisons. I learned quickly that there are two kinds of people you can't fool—a child and a sinner. I told the convicts that except for the grace of God I would be in prison, too. I told them that God still loved them and He was willing to save them.

One steamy, hot evening I preached in an all-Negro prison.

Two hundred of the four hundred men came to Christ after I had finished my message.

I went to a women's prison and talked to convicted murderers, dope addicts and forgers. Almost all of the 350 women came forth and rededicated their lives. One inmate, a strikingly beautiful girl, told me she had been the mistress of a dentist. She had been on narcotics and finally landed in prison for writing bad checks to support her addiction. She gave her life to Christ and after she was paroled she got a job, settled down and joined her church, completely abandoning the drugs and the promiscuous life she had led before.

Joyce now began to lose her doubts about my full Christian commitment. She and our two daughters gave their lives to the Lord, and Bible-reading, prayer and testimony became a regular part of our daily living. Christ was now the head of our household. Acts 16:31 became a reality in our home—"Believe on the Lord Jesus Christ, and thou shalt be saved, and thy house."

Word spread that I had renounced sin and made peace with the Lord. A friend called my wife and asked, "When can we hear Bob preach?" She replied, "Come by the house anytime, he's always going strong."

In those early days, my supercharged fervor for the Lord was even too much at times for Joyce. One Saturday morning I went with her to the beauty parlor. They gave her a haircut, a shampoo and then put her under the dryer. I went out for a walk, came back an hour later and asked the woman at the desk, "Excuse me, but do you have a saved lady in the salon?"

"What kind of lady?" she asked.

"A saved lady."

"Just a moment, please." She picked up a little intercom

system, switched on the microphone and her voice boomed
all over the shop: "Attention, everyone, attention. Do we have
a saved lady in the salon?"

My wife stuck her head out from under the dryer and
shouted, "Tell my fool husband I'll be there in a minute."

I preached next over Station WJDB in Thomasville, Alabama, and received a great deal of encouraging response. I
discovered that people were reacting to me, that they were
hungry for answers to their doubts, fears and problems.

My first revival took place at the Central Baptist Church
in Dixons Mills, Alabama. Up to this point, my message con-
sisted of telling how Christ had reached me and that if He
could come into my life, He could come into the lives of
others. I knew a few verses of the Bible—but my ignorance of
the Holy Book was still appalling. But, crude as my ministry
was, I nevertheless was winning souls by the hundreds.

Six months after my conversion, I was in Mobile speaking
to the skid-row denizens who visited the Rescue Mission
there. A call came from Dr. Bob Barker, pastor of the Chickasaw First Baptist Church. He said he wanted to baptize me.
I had to take a night off from my preaching, but I went
gratefully to the ancient rite of immersion. I felt cleansed and
purified and, if possible, my conviction for the Lord became
even stronger. Shortly after my baptism, I was officially
licensed by Dr. Barker's church as a "Minister of the Gospel
of the Lord Jesus Christ."

Then I received a letter from evangelist Eddie Martin,
who had heard me give my testimony in Laurel, Mississippi.
He said I was a "fervent soul-winner" and was sure I had
"the ability to organize." He offered me a job with his Team,
which would "mature you quickly in evangelism" and also
"satisfy your passion to win many lost souls to Christ."

I accepted eagerly and became advance man for the Eddie Martin Evangelistic Team. My job was to precede the Team into every town, arrange for publicity, talk with the sponsors of the revival and check out the churches where the revival would be held. As soon as this was done, I moved on to the next town to repeat the job. As promised, I did mature quickly in evangelism and the experience I gained was invaluable.

And wherever and whenever I could, I did some witnessing on the side. One late evening in Roanoke, Virginia, I found myself in an exclusive residential area and on impulse I walked up to the biggest house I saw. I rang the bell and a man answered.

"I'm Bob Harrington of the Eddie Martin Evangelistic Team, and I'm here to win your soul to Christ."

He slammed the door in my face.

Being a new Christian and not knowing any better, I wasn't discouraged. I rang the bell once more.

"You again?" he said, and this time he slammed the door even harder.

Then I kneeled on the porch and in a loud, thundering voice I began to pray for the soul of the hard-hearted man inside the house who refused to hear my message of salvation. Porch lights up and down the street began flickering on. Windows were raised and people were peering down at me. Suddenly the man inside the house swung the door open and declared in a fierce whisper, "Come on in, you fool, you're waking up all my neighbors."

I went inside and in fifteen minutes I had led the man to the Lord.

It was a good night's work and I felt that I had served God well.

After several months with Eddie Martin, I decided to strike out on my own. I had gained a good working knowledge of evangelistic fundamentals—how to organize and implement a revival. But I wasn't preaching enough, and my desire to shout my message from every platform I could find was overwhelming.

I had read that Jesus once told his disciples to go first to their own area and then to all the world, telling the gospel. I took that advice to heart and went back to Mobile.

I began by running an ad in the "Lost and Found" section of the Mobile *Press*. The ad said: "LOST? Are you wandering through life in the darkness of sin? I was until Jesus saved me. Call and let me tell you what Jesus did for me and how He can do the same for you." In one week, I had dozens of replies. And thirty-five people accepted Christ.

Then one day I saw a headline in the paper in large type: WOMAN FACES CHARGE IN STARVATION DEATH. The woman was in the county jail, accused of murdering her ten-month-old baby by withholding food from him. When I visited her at the jail, she readily confessed her guilt, although she had denied it before the authorities. She told me that after her husband disappeared she had taken to drink. Her baby had starved because she spent all her money on alcohol. I told her of the love that Jesus had for her, despite her brutal crime. We prayed together and I asked God to save her sinful soul. She came to the Lord and I counseled with her all through her trial. She told me of the great change in her attitude since her salvation and that she was reading her Bible and how burdened she was for all the other women in the jail who had not experienced a new birth in Jesus.

After serving a five-year sentence, she was released. She remarried and raised a new family of three children. I still hear from her. She hasn't taken a drink since she was saved and she is living a good, happy, joy-filled Christian life, completely rehabilitated because of her love for God.

In Mobile I continued to preach at every opportunity—in the jail, at the Rescue Mission, before social and fraternal clubs, in churches, schools and private homes. Every time I rode in an elevator I preached too. (Nothing a soul-winner likes more than a captive audience.) I'd ask my fellow passengers, "Which way will your last trip be, up or down?" If someone said he wanted to be saved, I'd press the emergency button and hold the elevator right there till I won him for the Lord.

Then support for my ministry came unexpectedly from the Mobile Christian Businessmen's Committee, a layman's group dedicated to winning souls. One of the committee's most influential men was Fred Roan, a successful automobile dealer. He helped me organize a revival and on the day of the meeting the public square was filled to overflowing. After I preached, many of the city's outstanding businessmen gave their testimony. They told what Jesus had done for them and how thankful they were for salvation. Many in the crowd were inspired. More than one hundred pressed forward and gave their lives to Christ.

One day, Fred and I went to a large Mobile cafeteria for lunch. Over five hundred people were there, many of them preachers who were in town for a state evangelistic conference. Fred said to me, "Why don't you give your testimony here?" Bold as I was, I felt a wave of embarrassment overcome me. How could I stand up before a relaxed lunchtime gathering in a public restaurant and assert myself before such a large group of people?

Fred didn't wait for my answer. He began to tap loudly on his glass with a knife. "Your attention, please," he said. Everyone stopped right where they were. Conversation died. "I have a friend here," Fred continued, "who is going to tell you about his experience with the Lord."

The huge room became silent and every eye turned toward me.

I got up on a chair and somehow I lost my embarrassment and the words began to flow. I told of my personal experience with Christ and the new life He had given me. Then I asked for a show of hands of all those who also had discovered living in Christ was a boundlessly uplifting experience. Dozens of hands went up. "Those of you who raised your hands turn to your neighbors who didn't and tell them how they, too, can be saved." I concluded with a short prayer and sat down. There was stillness for a long moment—then suddenly a wave of spontaneous applause rippled through the room. It was the first time I had been applauded for preaching the gospel and it proved to me that a man should never, no matter what the circumstances, be afraid or timid about bringing the good news of Jesus. Only later did I learn that the restaurant's cashier had phoned the police and reported, "There's a crazy man in here, he's standing on a chair and ranting away about God. You've got to stop him." Two policemen had arrived while I was giving my testimony, but, instead of interrupting me, they listened to what I was saying and after I concluded they had joined in the applause. They came over and congratulated me. One of them said, "We certainly can't charge you with disturbing the peace for preaching about God."

"Amen," I said.

The policemen joined our table and by the time the meal was finished both had promised to rededicate their lives to Christ.

Next I went on television to conduct an all-day "Soul-A-Thon," the first of its kind in Mobile. I talked about how I had changed from a man hustling for the almighty dollar to a man dedicated to "hustling" for God. We had people on who gave their testimony, special music, a choir. Thousands of telephone calls, telegrams and letters streamed in as a result of the program and hundreds were won to Christ.

Raising money to keep my ministry going began to be a problem. All through my stay in Mobile there was never enough cash on hand to implement my ambitious plans for bringing the Lord's word to all the people who desperately needed it. Joyce had taken a job teaching school, and many of my bills were paid from her small salary. I also prayed frequently for support and somehow the Lord provided, though I was still only one step ahead of the bill collectors.

I had been preaching for a year—"saved three hundred and sixty-five days," I told an audience, "and never happier"—when I organized a Crusade for Souls. The Crusade opened in a large drive-in movie theater outside the city, the first such service ever held in Mobile, and it was an instant success, despite the unusual surroundings. The service was heard in the cars over the same individual loudspeakers used to pipe in the sound track of movies. When I finished my message I called on those who had decided for Christ to flick their headlights on and come forward. Like a squadron of fireflies, lights went on all over the huge parking area and close to one hundred people gave their lives to the Lord.

Then I extended the Crusade to tents and churches and began getting invitations from other cities—including Chickasaw, Linden and Demopolis, Alabama. In the Linden Crusade, the last two weeks of the meeting were held in the county courthouse. More people were saved and I continued to thrive in God's work.

Also, I was beginning to win some recognition for my soulwinning:

From the Alabama *Baptist:* "People came forth in large numbers for prayers, and the third night of the meeting there were over thirty professions of faith and over fifty who came for re-dedication. Tears of joy were witnessed at the lost being saved and Christians demonstrating a brotherly love toward one another. Hate was turned into love and the assembly sang deep meaningful hymns. Reverend Harrington preached moving messages centered in the Scriptures. Each night after his demonstration of God's presence the revival deepened. As the invitation was given, so many came forward that room had to be provided for them to stand in front of the pulpit."

From R. H. Bounds, probate judge of Clarke County, Alabama: "I recommend the Reverend Harrington to every county in the state. After his soul-winning revival, our county will never be the same."

From Mrs. Maxine Martin of Mobile: "When I hear this evangelist, Bob Harrington, and his bold preaching, I think of John the Baptist and his compassion for the lost and his preaching of Christ-like living."

From Reverend Cosby Hall, pastor: "Bob's preaching style makes one think of the late Billy Sunday. However, Bob is unique in his presentation of the Gospel and he can captivate the attention of his audience."

From Stanley Dunegan, converted in one of the Crusades: "Last night after hearing evangelist Bob Harrington and accepting Jesus as my Lord and Savior, my old life went out and my new life came in. I thank God for a man who makes salvation so easily understood."

From Reverend M. M. Harvison, pastor: "Bob is a fearless, powerful preacher of the Gospel of Jesus Christ. See and hear this man and you'll never be the same."

From C. R. Myrick, Mayor of Coffeeville, Alabama: "Coffeeville thanks Bob Harrington for coming to our city. With the leadership and blessing of our Lord, a spiritual awakening has come to us. As mayor I would recommend this team to your church and city."

Without my realizing it, the recognition I was beginning to win was also putting my family in jeopardy. One night while I was out preaching, a prowler tried to break into our Chickasaw apartment while Joyce and the girls were sleeping.

"This is the home of Satan," the man screamed from outside as he tried to claw his way through a screen door.

Frantic, Joyce shouted, "If you come in that door, I'll shoot you." It was a bluff—there wasn't a gun in the house.

"Satan saves! Satan saves!" the apparently demented intruder kept repeating while my family remained terrorized.

Joyce dialed the police and they arrived in time to chase off the crazed man. A week later he was caught. The police told us the unfortunate man was a narcotics addict with a $40-a-day heroin habit.

I stayed in Chickasaw long enough to calm Joyce and the children down after their harrowing experience and to conduct a campaign against a newly formed country club. When I heard that some of the town's leading citizens were planning to finance the club—they had even given two Baptist ministers honorary memberships—I went on the warpath. The promoters claimed the club would provide "healthy relaxation" in the form of golf for the men, bridge parties for the women and a swimming pool for the children. But I had been in enough country clubs to know the sinful atmosphere generated in such surroundings—drinking, gambling and infidelity.

I went on the radio and lambasted the project. I gave the names of those who were behind it—and challenged them to contribute their money to the Lord instead of the devil.

My broadcast created a furor. Pledges were quickly withdrawn and plans for the club were as quickly abandoned. To this day, Chickasaw doesn't have a country club, thanks to the campaign I initiated.

There was a great deal of soul-winning to be done in Chickasaw. And I was still so in rapture with the Lord that I made it my business every chance I got to challenge complacency and hypocrisy head-on—even among those who considered themselves devout Christians.

One Sunday morning while Joyce and I were entering the First Baptist Church I accosted a woman in her sixties, her face smeared unbecomingly with rouge and lipstick, her body wrapped in a tight girdle.

"Are you saved?" I challenged.

She was shocked at the question. She looked me over as though I was an emissary from the devil. Then, regaining her composure, she puffed, "Young man, I'll have you know that I was saved years before you were born."

"You don't look like a saved Christian to me," I answered.

She turned on her heel and stalked away.

I looked at Joyce, who was blushing furiously. "Do you know who that was?" she asked. "She's the president of the Women's Missionary Union."

"Doesn't matter," I added firmly. "She still looks like she needs saving."

Meantime, I literally gave my life to the Lord at every opportunity. Each Sunday, the pastor at the First Baptist Church would extend an invitation for rededication. I was always the first one down the aisle to pledge renewed faith in the God I had so recently found. I didn't know you weren't supposed to keep rededicating yourself. One day a church deacon asked me, "Why do you keep giving your life to Christ each time the pastor extends an invitation?" I looked him squarely in the eye and answered, "So I won't get like you, soft and slothful in my battle for Jesus."

I thought he was going to faint. He walked away from me glassy-eyed, a hurt expression on his face.

I had hit a nerve—he knew it and I knew it. But instead of the incident ending our friendship, it resulted in the deacon's following my example and renewing his faith in God each time the invitation was given. A few weeks after I had so impetuously accused him, he gave his testimony from the pulpit, recounting our conversation, then adding: "Thank God for Christians like Bob Harrington. If it wasn't for Bob I would still be living outside the kingdom of heaven. He showed me how to be a true believer." He still tells the story often, and by this time I imagine he's given his life to Christ several hundred times.

To spread the faith, I bought an old furniture van and had a huge sign painted on the side: BOB HARRINGTON'S GOSPEL WAGON. REMEMBER, THE WAGES OF SIN IS DEATH.

I knew that close to Chickasaw, in the small community of Saraland, population about 5,000, there was a pocket of sin that was notorious all over Alabama. The mayor had been assassinated, cut down by bullets from an unknown assailant in his own backyard. Dozens of main-street honky-tonks flourished, selling dope, booze and girls.

Rolling up in my gospel wagon one day, I got on the speaker and began denouncing the sin in the community. I was preaching across the street from the town's most infamous nightclub. I declared that the mayor's assassin was known, that the town was a modern Sodom, and I spelled out the names of the clubs where dope could be purchased.

That night two deputies knocked at my door, one of them tall and sandy-haired, the other short and sporting a crew cut.

"Does Bob Harrington live here?" the tall one asked.

I introduced myself. I thought the two men were under conviction and wanted to be saved.

"We understand you know who killed the mayor," the short deputy said.

"I know who does know."

They poised their pencils, ready to jot down the name.

"God knows!"

"God knows everything," the tall deputy said.

"Glad to hear you admit that. Whoever killed the mayor heard me today and he realizes God knows he's guilty. The Holy Spirit is working on him, rest assured of that."

The smaller of the two men said, "You've got a lot of courage coming into town and stirring up a hornet's nest."

I explained that I had no fear because I was right with the Lord. I said, "No point in you men wasting this trip. While you're here, you can get right with the Lord yourselves."

The tall man immediately gave his heart to Jesus and the other man rededicated his life.

As they were leaving, the sandy-haired deputy said he had been assigned to me as a full-time bodyguard. "We saw someone in the crowd today with a rifle and we want to be sure that what happened to the mayor doesn't happen to you."

I told him I didn't need a bodyguard. The Lord would protect me. "Just the same," he said, "we don't want a preacher shot in the back. Anything could happen in Saraland."

My campaign soon began to pay off. Owners of the joints I had named where dope was on sale called and threatened me. One of them, particularly irate, asked me why I had mentioned his place. "Everybody in town knows about it," I answered. "I thought I'd just give you a little free advertising." He slammed the receiver down, a curse on his lips.

I kept hammering away. Amazingly, there were hundreds of folks in Saraland who were fed up with the corruption and sin in their town. Word was quietly passed that the town was fortunate to have a hell-raising preacher to stir things up.

Business now began to fall off at the honky-tonks. The club across the street from where I was preaching closed down. So did several others. The traffic in dope began to dry up. A Civic Betterment Society was organized by many of the town's leading citizens and the mayor was ousted. A new mayor, pledged to a clean-up administration, was elected. A new ordinance was passed to toughen the requirements for operating a bar. To this day, the spiritual and civic atmosphere in Saraland is a far cry from what it once was. I don't give myself undue credit for this regeneration, but I know, too, that if a lone man hadn't preached God's mighty word from a furniture van turned into a gospel wagon, Saraland would still be wallowing in the stench and stink of sin and evil.

I moved the gospel wagon to Mobile and there I pulled up in front of another gaudy set of honky-tonks. Complaints about my preaching against the evils of drink bombarded the authorities. One policeman came around and told me to "take it easy." I wouldn't take it easy, and held my meetings regularly, though I was forced to move the wagon several times because owners wouldn't permit me to use their property. The Book of Acts tells how the disciples Paul and Silas were put in jail. Nowadays you're supposed to have freedom of speech and religion so they can't put you in jail—but you can be ostracized and tagged, as I was, a nut, an extremist, a rightist and a leftist.

I wasn't intimidated. I continued to preach, knowing that God was preparing and shaping me for future tribulations.

A call suddenly came for me to preach at a revival in Pensacola, Florida. The call wasn't from a church. At this point in my ministry, it was still difficult for me to get church sponsorship. Pastors and church leaders opposed me as a "flamboyant radical." But a group of Christian businessmen in Pensacola led by Clarence Taylor invited me down and asked me to bring my message.

Billboards with my picture sprouted all over town. Newspapers carried long stories about the revival I was going to lead. I was given radio and television time (after one broadcast I led the announcer and one of the cameramen to the Lord). On the TV stage we had eight telephones set up so people could call in and ask questions, be saved or have their spiritual life renewed. The "Soul-A-Thon" was a huge success, and thousands of people were inspired by it.

Outside town we set up a tent that would hold 2,500 people and the crowds were tremendous. Civic leaders and businessmen got up and gave their testimony, telling what the Savior had done to change their lives. During each service, pastors and laymen gathered on the sawdust floor of the huge tent, fell on their knees and cried out for the saving presence of Christ to be felt in their city. Their prayers were answered.

The crowds became so large that we had to move to the city auditorium. In all, 754 people were saved, and I was heartened by this outpouring of faith.

Two pastors came forward and declared publicly what the impact of the revival had meant to Pensacola.

The Reverend A. R. Kingman said: "I want to thank Bob Harrington for his appearance here. Many of our people have quit 'playing church' and have gone to work for the Lord. God has given Reverend Harrington a unique ability to make Christians realize how far short they are of the goal, and to want to do something about it."

The Reverend Bertie Singletary added: "In these days of sin and compromise inside the church, I can think of no greater message than that which Brother Bob Harrington fearlessly preaches—that of salvation, separation and soul-winning. During his revival our church was awakened and the city of Pensacola stirred. I count it a privilege to be able to recommend Brother Bob as a man whose life is dedicated to winning the lost, and whose preaching has been a demonstration of the power of the Holy Spirit."

Before I left Pensacola, the entire city was stirred by the conversion of two outstanding businessmen.

Ralph Jordon, a wealthy tile dealer, called me and I arranged to meet him at his warehouse. He poured out the unhappy story of his experience with Christ. As a young boy he had asked God to leave him alone—and seemingly God had honored his request. Now the man was haunted by the fear that God would never visit him again.

I reassured him that Christ was always ready to save a transgressor, that God indeed could visit him again, not once, but for the rest of his life. In his warehouse—surrounded by a million dollars worth of tile—Ralph Jordan and I got down on our knees and I brought him to the Lord.

J. D. Wallace, along with his eight-year-old daughter, had strayed into my revival—thinking it was a circus. After hearing my message, he approached me and said he was at the breaking point. He was suffering business reverses and his nerves were so shot that he had found himself one day on the highway banging his head against the steering wheel of his car.

I talked to him about the power of Jesus, and on the kitchen floor of a local Baptist church, he, too, gave his heart to the Lord.

All of Pensacola was moved when J. D. Wallace gave his testimony on television the next day. Since he's been saved, each Christmas he sends his customers Bibles instead of bottles of booze and he calls me every year on his spiritual birthday.

Pensacola had been the high point, thus far, of my ministry. I had been preaching for two years—a babe in Christ who had converted more than five thousand souls. But I still felt I was ignorant of theology and that I needed intellectual seasoning to continue my work for the Lord.

5

THE MIDDLE OF HELL

I was accepted as a student at the New Orleans Baptist Theological Seminary. Almost penniless, Joyce, Rhonda, Mitzi and I arrived in the queen city of the Mississippi in an old, broken-down Dodge.

Luckily, Joyce got a teaching job at a public school as I began my studies.

Though I had two tempestuous years of evangelizing behind me, I knew little of formal Christianity.

I learned the rituals and the stormy yet inspiring history of the Baptist Church. I was particularly thrilled by the lives of four great evangelists, Jesus, Roger Williams, who founded the first Baptist church on American soil, and those two great modern-day preachers, Billy Sunday and Billy Graham.

While reading the Book of Luke, I found to my surprise that Jesus had only begun to preach after he was thirty. Somehow this seemed especially significant to me, for I had been just past thirty when my call to spread the gospel had come.

In three short years Jesus had changed the world for all time to come. What impressed me most about His life was that He taught that God loved and forgave sinners and that repentance and faith could save men. Jesus fought sin, particularly hypocrisy and cruelty to the weak. He didn't despise sinners and He believed that God's power was greater than sin. Without being fully aware of it, I had been following the teachings of Jesus in my own efforts to save souls. And though I didn't know it at the time, I would shortly be carrying out His principles in my ministry to sinners on Bourbon Street.

Roger Williams had witnessed unspeakable cruelty perpetrated in the name of religion. Like myself, he was the son of a storekeeper. At the age of eighteen he was appointed recording secretary in Britain's infamous Court of the Star Chamber and he saw men, women and children accused as heretics, tortured and hanged. Even dissenting clergymen were not exempt from the most horrible punishment. Dr. Alexander Leighton, a minister who had clashed with the Church of England, was stripped of his vestments, publicly whipped, had his nostrils split, his ears cut off and was imprisoned for life. When Williams began to fearlessly preach the doctrine of separation of church and state, an order for his arrest was issued. He escaped to America, accepted a pastorate in Salem, Massachusetts, made friends with the Indians, then established the colony of Providence with the important stipulation that the government should hold sway only in civil affairs and that all men must be free to worship, or not to worship, as they chose. Quakers, Puritans, Congregationalists and Jews flocked to Providence, and a century and a half later Williams' pioneer fight influenced the Founding Fathers to guarantee freedom of religion in the first amendment to the Constitution.

Billy Sunday wasn't a Baptist, but he inspired many Baptist ministers to become evangelists. "I want to be a giant for God," he declared in ringing sermons at three hundred revivals throughout the United States. An ex-baseball player, Billy, during his twenty-nine-year career as a sinbuster, was controversial, sensational and unorthodox in his methods—but he got results. He preached to more than a hundred million people and converted at least one million.

Billy Graham's evangelical star was rising swiftly while I was studying at the seminary. His fantastic success in his world-wide Crusades made him my idol and a constant source of inspiration.

I, too, wanted to shake the world for Christ, but there was the more immediate and practical problem of supplementing Joyce's earnings and helping to provide for my family.

I dared myself to dream big. Where and to whom could I go to work most effectively for the Lord? In New Orleans there was only one place and one man.

Without references or letters of introduction, I decided to apply to Dr. J. D. Grey, pastor of the 4,000-member First Baptist Church and a past president of the Southern Baptist Convention.

I got into our car on the afternoon I had made up my mind to see Dr. Grey. I turned on the ignition, but the car wouldn't start. I was out of gas, and didn't have enough money to fill the tank. To get to the church, I hopped a bus and then transferred to a trolley.

I sat in Dr. Grey's outer office for two hours. I had no appointment and wasn't at all sure he would see me. Then, finally, he came to the door, looked me over, and inquired crisply, "Young man, what can I do for you?"

I remembered Billy Sunday's words. "I want to be a giant for God," I heard myself saying.

Dr. Grey ushered me into his office. "If your qualifications match your ambition, we might have something to talk about," he said.

He listened intently while I gave my testimony and told him about my experience in evangelism. "I'm living in the joy

of the Holy Spirit," I concluded, "but I have to find something
to do to support my family while I'm in school."

"You've found it," he declared to my astonishment. "You
can be my assistant here at the church."

He offered me a small salary, but, more important, he was
giving me a chance to work alongside him.

I barely had enough money for the bus and trolley trip
home. When I told Joyce the news, she rejoiced with me. We
got down on our knees and prayed. Joyce had been more
frightened about our move to New Orleans than I realized.
In her prayer, she gave thanks that God had opened another
door for us in a strange city far from home where we had no
friends.

I became a workhorse for the church. No sacrifice was too
great, no job too demanding. I led a week-long youth revival
in which many lives were changed and hearts were warmed.
I helped keep the church records, made hospital visits and
evangelistic calls and dealt with those who responded to the
invitation at the conclusion of services. Dr. Grey often called
me his Timothy—a reference to the martyr who had been
converted by Saint Paul and who had been his trusted friend
and companion.

Dr. Grey had a powerful influence on me. I abandoned
my crew cut and began to wear my hair long, as he did. I
adopted his frankness in my preaching, imitated his speed-
demon delivery and his quick side-to-side movements in the
pulpit.

"I'll make a real preacher out of you," Dr. Grey had
promised, and he was true to his word.

After several months at First Baptist, I asked Dr. Grey if I
could be ordained into the church's ministry.

He agreed at once, and, shortly after, I was issued my
precious certificate of ordination: "We, the undersigned,

hereby certify that upon the recommendation and request of the First Baptist Church at New Orleans, Louisiana, which had full and sufficient opportunity for judging of his gifts, and after satisfactory examination by us in regard to his Christian experience, call to the ministry and view of Bible Doctrine, Bob Harrington, who, has been solemnly and publicly set apart and ordained to the work of The Gospel Ministry on this 8th day of February, 1961."

The first signature on my ordination certificate was that of Dr. Grey. Many of my teachers from the seminary and friends from Sweet Water, Mobile and Chickasaw attended the ceremony that formally made me a preacher. It was an impressive service, and deacons, reverends, professors and other learned men of the church took part in the "laying on of hands." I took a look around at all the Ph.D.s and D.D.s and remarked jestingly: "Our churches have so many doctors that you would think God was sick."

I began preaching all over New Orleans—to the B'nai B'rith, Rotary, on street corners, in private homes, churches, anywhere I could find an audience. Dr. Grey said of me: "Bob has preached everywhere in New Orleans except the St. Louis Cathedral, and I think he's trying to get permission from the Pope to hold a meeting there."

One day Dr. Grey sent me to the French Quarter to visit a successful businessman who had abandoned the church and was divorcing his wife. He was living with a prostitute and intended to marry her. I talked with this middle-aged man, father of four children, and begged him to come to his senses. But he assured me he was happy and knew exactly what he was doing. I used all my powers of persuasion, but couldn't budge him back onto the path of righteousness. Leaving his apartment, I realized that I could have reached him if I had only gotten to him sooner. I began thinking that God needed a witness on Bourbon Street.

A few days later, in chapel, I heard Dr. Leo Eddleman, president of the seminary, say something that really hit home. "Wherever there is a pocket of sin, there is a mission field—and the nearest Christian to it is a missionary."

Starting with Simon Peter and his brother Andrew, Jesus has called disciples of every generation to be fishers of men. What bigger fishing hole could a preacher have than Bourbon Street? I'd never run out of prospects.

I decided to open a "Salvation Shop" in the heart of the French Quarter—the area that Billy Graham, during a visit there, had called "the middle of hell."

The ten city blocks that made up the French Quarter are Satan's lair, perhaps the most sin-soaked thoroughfares in the world. Tiny book stores openly display pornography. Marijuana, heroin, cocaine and LSD are brazenly peddled by pushers. Sex orgies, often with more than a dozen men and women participating, take place behind the closed shutters of fashionable apartments with French wrought-iron balconies. There are bars frequented only by homosexuals. Others cater solely to lesbians. Drinking is an around-the-clock pastime since New Orleans is the only city in America that has no curfew on its bars. Teen-age girls, runaways from home and out of money, solicit on the streets, giving the established professional prostitutes unwanted competition. And everywhere are the strip joints. There's enough bumping and grinding to start an earthquake.

Because of the licentiousness of the French Quarter, someone has called New Orleans "the city that Care has forgotten." It's an apt observation. For centuries the churches have remained silent and winked at the public display of depravity in all its most virulent forms. And among the most disgusting things I've seen in the Quarter are ministers and priests in clerical garb reeling through the streets dead drunk.

I had set myself a formidable task. I was still studying at the seminary and tending to my duties at the First Baptist Church. But I determined that, come what may, I was going to bring the Lord's word to this "pocket of sin."

What's more, I wanted the sinners to see me coming from blocks away. I wasn't going to pussyfoot around. To call attention to myself, I adopted the custom of wearing a red tie, red pocket handkerchief and red socks. And I carried with me everywhere a Bible bound in red leather. Those are my trademarks to this day.

I began exploring Bourbon Street, trying to find a location for my Salvation Shop. The reactions of renting agents and landlords ranged from jeers to laughter. One club owner told me that he would personally see to it that no preacher would set up anywhere in the French Quarter.

When I told Dr. Grey of my plans, he counseled caution. "You can't just go out there and grab the world by the neck and shove Christ down the throats of people who want no part of Him. Stay where you are and you can reach more sinners than if you locate on Bourbon Street."

I told him, "I feel a deep calling. I'm sure this is what God wants me to do."

"Then," he advised, "use strategy. 'Be as wise as a serpent, as harmless as a dove.'"

Joyce encouraged my foray into the French Quarter. "If the Lord has told you to minister on Bourbon Street, you'd better get down there fast." She remembered how exciting night life had been to me before my conversion and knew I could talk and understand the language of the honky-tonk habitués. "Maybe you can help some husbands be the kind of men their wives would admire and respect," she said.

The next morning I set out again, determined to find a location. But I didn't see a single "For Rent" sign. Then, near trumpeter Al Hirt's place, I noticed a storefront with barred windows. I tried the door. It was locked. From a janitor working in the nearby Dixieland Jazz Hall, I learned that the owner was a man named T. J. Dalbora. I went to see him.

"Just what do you plan to do with the location?" he asked.

"I'm going to open a way station for lost souls."

"What sort of reaction do you expect?"

"I don't know what response to anticipate. I don't know whether people in the Quarter will think of me as a friend or an enemy. They may view me as a holier-than-thou preacher coming to point a finger at them, or as a friend coming to bind the wounds of sin."

"I've had everything from a tattoo parlor to a package liquor store in that location. Why not an evangelist?"

He wouldn't give me a long-term lease. If he thought that a preacher couldn't afford to make a financial commitment of any duration, he was right as far as my funds were concerned. Or perhaps he thought I wouldn't last more than a short time. At any rate, we agreed on a weekly rent of seventy-five dollars.

Now I was really on Bourbon Street, across the street from the Dixieland Jazz Hall and the Circus Club, which featured strippers. I was just three doors from Al Hirt's trumpet and one block from Pete Fountain's clarinet.

The day I opened was an exciting one. I moved in a desk and chair. But I didn't have a secretary or a telephone. I set up a Bible display in the window and to the weather-beaten front door I tacked an invitation, "Come in." Outside I hung a cross, painted red.

My only visitor that day was the tragic Sunbeam. In the days that followed, curious barkers, strippers, tourists, drifters, drunks, homosexuals, narcotics addicts and prostitutes wandered in—most of them only to take a look at "the nutty preacher" who had invaded Bourbon Street.

I brought our stereo unit from home and secured one speaker to the front door. I played hymns all day long—a strange counterpoint to the brassy, provocative music that surged from the strip joints all around me.

The barker for the Circus Club began paying attention to me. "You didn't come down here to go to church, now did you?" he shouted to passers-by. "If you've got to go see that hairy preacher, be sure to come in here first so you'll have some real sin for him to forgive." (Two months later this same barker came to me and gave his life to Jesus.)

Next to the Circus Club stood a four-story apartment building. Shortly after I opened, the owner of the building came to see me. "Preacher," he said, "my wife and kids are starving at home because of this fool religious music you're blasting into the street. I'll give you twenty dollars a week if you'll turn the music off."

"Sorry, I can't do it," I said.

"But nobody wants to rent a place where they have to listen all day to 'The Old Rugged Cross.'"

Several weeks later the man's building was raided by District Attorney Jim Garrison's vice squad. The place had been a front for illegal gambling and prostitution.

One club owner, later indicted as a kingpin in the Louisiana Mafia and notorious in the Quarter for the lewdness of the acts performed in his club, kept pressure on me during the first month. Night after night he would tear down my display of tracts attached to the window where the Bible was on display. Day after day I replaced the tracts, and added a sign in my window that said: "May I Help You?" His pressure finally abated one day when he heard me preaching on the street to a large crowd. He told me, "If you can attract that many people, I'll fire one of my strippers and hire you."

On another occasion, while I was preaching in front of a particularly seedy strip club, the bartender came out and spilled a glass of beer over my head. The beer trickled onto the pages of my Bible. I felt like pounding that man into the blacktop, but I remembered the words of Christ . . . "whosoever shall smite thee on thy right cheek, turn to him the other also."

Despite all the opposition, I was beginning to make an impact on Bourbon Street. The owner of the Circus Club let me preach on Sunday afternoons from the same stage where his strippers pranced. But before I could build a following, District Attorney Garrison, spearheading a clean-up drive, began raiding some of the Quarter's strip joints. The Circus Club's proprietor thought I was in league with Garrison and he refused to let me continue my preaching.

I had made a dent in Bourbon Street. But my progress was painfully slow until I decided to confront and challenge the man who was reputed to be the most influential gangland figure in Louisiana.

6

THE CONVERSION OF
CARLOS MARCELLO

Ever since I came to New Orleans, I had been reading
newspaper and magazine stories about Carlos Marcello, a
stocky, barrel-chested man of tremendous wealth, and his
court battles against unsuccessful government attempts to declare him an undesirable alien and to deport him.

The stories I read had few words of kindness about him.
Even his gifts to charity—including a reported $100,000 be-
quest to agencies helping victims made homeless by a hurri-
cane and a $10,000 contribution to the Girl Scouts—were
dismissed as empty gestures or a payoff of "conscience money."

Yet I wondered if the man could really be as evil as his
reputation and—even more—if a man like Marcello could be
induced to come to the Lord. It would be a daring, un-
precedented achievement for a young, unknown evangelist.

There were obvious obstacles. Carlos Marcello had never
heard of me. We were of different faiths. In background
and temperament, we had nothing in common. Would he see
me? Would he listen to me? And there was the ultimate
question—was the message of Christ strong enough to touch
the heart of this man?

But I knew if Christ were in my place, He would not

falter. Gaining courage from that realization, I decided to test my power as a soul-winner against a man whose soul according to some was already committed to hell.

Having made up my mind, how was I to meet Marcello? I couldn't just walk up to his front door and introduce myself. No doubt he employed bodyguards whose job it was to protect him from strangers. I needed an intermediary.

I began by asking every church official I met if he knew Marcello. I was answered with scornful, puzzled and contemptuous stares. Some of the churchman I questioned hurried off, terror in their eyes at the mere mention of the name of Carlos Marcello.

Finally, at a small suburban church where I was leading a revival, I talked with one of the deacons, Tom Prude. He told me he was a draftsman for a contractor who built houses and hotels for Marcello.

"Can you arrange an appointment for me with Marcello?" I asked Prude.

The surprise showed clearly in his face. But he said calmly, "Let me see what I can do."

"Tell him," I urged, "that I want to see him about Jesus. I want him to get saved and give his heart to the Lord, to see that Christ is the answer to his needs and problems. And tell him I'm not looking for a handout."

I wanted to make it perfectly clear I had no financial motive. Ninety per cent of the time, clergymen who contact wealthy laymen end up asking for a contribution.

Days passed, then weeks. I was beginning to doubt that I would ever get to Marcello.

Then I received a phone call from Tom Prude. He told me that it was arranged—I could see Marcello the next morning at eight o'clock at his home.

Wild thoughts now began to race through my mind.

Marcello had actually agreed to see me. But why? For laughs? For sport? So he could mock God?

Trying to calm my restlessness, I switched on the television set to watch a movie. It didn't help my nervousness any when the film turned out to be *Scarface,* the blood-soaked Hollywood version of Al Capone's murderous career in Chicago.

Joyce decided not to work the next day. Instead, she gathered five other seminary wives, and they all spent the morning praying for me—and Marcello.

I didn't sleep a wink that night. And because I anticipated complete rejection by Marcello, I read and reread the passages in my seminary textbooks which told how to overcome the objections of a sinner and lead him to God. When morning finally came, I was too jumpy to touch my breakfast.

Tom Prude rolled up in his car at seven-thirty. I didn't even know how to get to Marcello's house. He said, "You follow me, and I'll lead you to Marcello's place. When we get there, I'll leave. Then you'll be alone with him."

I found myself driving behind Prude, and shortly we reached the most fashionable suburb of New Orleans, a crescent of houses bordering an exclusive country club. Prude pulled up to a columned home that was easily worth $100,000. He pointed at the house, then drove on.

I went up the walkway and rang the bell. I heard the sound of chimes echoing inside the house. It was too late to turn and run now. After a long moment, a short, stocky man with gray temples and wearing a white shirt came to the door. He was casually looping his belt into his blue trousers.

"I'm Reverend Bob Harrington. I'm here to see Mr. Marcello," I said as boldly as I could.

"I'm Marcello," the man said.

He asked me to come in. He looked as distinguished as a banker and there wasn't a bodyguard in sight.

We walked through a hallway hung with paintings into a large living room. There was a Steinway baby grand piano in one corner and thick, soft, luxurious white carpeting that gave you the illusion of floating on air. We sat down on a small couch in front of a marble-topped coffee table.

"I was told you wanted to talk to me about God," Marcello said quietly.

"I want to tell you about a simple plan of salvation," I began.

He looked at me with interest, his eyes alert and questioning.

"Do you believe the Lord loves you?"

"If anybody does, it would have to be the Lord."

I took out a small pocket Bible and turned to Romans 3:23. "'For all have sinned, and come short of the glory of God,'" I read aloud. "Do you believe that you're a sinner?"

"I know I am."

I was shocked at Marcello's answer. To convince him that he was living outside the grace of God, I was ready to repeat all the charges made against him by the government and the press. The last thing I expected was his simple straightforward admission that he was a sinner.

"I want you to realize that the Lord will forgive your sins. The only difference between us is not my goodness and your badness, but the fact that Jesus lives in my heart. He has saved my soul."

"Tell me some more."

"You read this next verse," I said, pointing to Romans 6:23.

He took the Bible and in a slightly accented voice he

recited: "'For the wages of sin is death; but the gift of God is eternal life through Jesus Christ our Lord.'"

I had him holding and reading the Bible. It was another encouraging sign. Quickly, I went on to explain the passage. "That means that if you keep living in sin without Jesus, you're going to be paid off with eternal spiritual death. Not only you, but everyone in the world who dies without Christ. The penalty of sin *is* death. Which would you rather have, death or eternal life?"

"I'd rather have life."

"Then you have to allow Jesus to come into your heart."

"Show me some more."

I took the Bible and found the next verse I wanted him to hear, Romans 10:9. "That if thou shalt confess with thy mouth the Lord Jesus, and shalt believe in thine heart that God hath raised him from the dead, thou shalt be saved."

"I'm not sure I understand that."

"I didn't either until I got saved. It means that if you want Jesus to become your Lord, you have to accept Him through your mouth and heart. The mouth and heart work together. Out of the mouth come the things that are in a person's heart. When a man has a dirty mouth, he's got an evil heart. When a man uses cheap words, he has cheap thoughts in his heart. The mouth is the broadcasting station and dispatch office of the heart."

"I've never heard it put that way before. It makes sense."

"Mr. Marcello, do you believe that Jesus died for you?"

"If it says that in the Bible, I believe it."

"Do you believe the Lord meant it when He said that if you let Him into your heart, He will save your soul?"

"Yes."

"Let's look at Romans 10:10. 'For with the heart man

believeth unto righteousness; and with the mouth confession is made unto salvation.' Do you believe that, too?"

"I'm trying."

"Do you believe the Bible to be the word of God?"

"I have no reason not to. My family believed it. I believed it when I was young and I believe it now."

"Do you believe Romans 10:13?" I read aloud, "For whosoever shall call upon the name of the Lord shall be saved."

"Does that mean it's not too late for *me* to be saved?"

"Two years ago," I said, "I couldn't have helped you, Mr. Marcello. I thought then the gulf between a Catholic and a Baptist was too great. But I've learned that Jesus offers salvation to all men."

Now I asked the most crucial question of all. "Are you willing to trust the Lord as your personal Savior—right here and right at this moment?"

"Yes, I am."

I couldn't have been more surprised. Carlos Marcello was coming to the Lord. He had been the least difficult of all the people I had rescued for Christ. I had been prepared for any objection he might raise, any reluctance, any doubt. What I had forgotten was that the Spirit of God, while He was preparing me to witness to this man, was also preparing him. God works in many ways.

"Do you know how to pray?"

"No."

"Let's get down on our knees."

I kneeled in front of the couch. So did he.

"Now give me your hand as a sign that you want Jesus to come into your heart. If you really are willing to repent, you'll give me your hand."

Without hesitation he placed his hand in mine.

"Are you ready to pray?"

"I'm ready."

I asked him to bow his head and repeat after me:

"Thank you, Lord, for loving us."

"Thank you, Lord, for loving us."

"Thank you for giving your life for sinners like us."

"Thank you for giving your life for sinners like us."

"Dear Lord, come into my heart."

"Dear Lord, come into my heart."

"Forgive my sins and save my soul."

"Forgive my sins and save my soul."

"I believe in you, Lord, as my Savior and Master."

"I believe in you, Lord, as my Savior and Master."

"Thank you, Lord, for dying for me and help me, Lord, to live for you."

"Thank you, Lord, for dying for me and help me, Lord, to live for you."

"Thank you, Lord Jesus, for saving my soul. Amen."

"Thank you, Lord Jesus, for saving my soul. Amen."

When we stood up there were tears in Marcello's eyes. "I'll never forget what you've done for me," he said.

I circled the verses I had quoted and gave him the Bible. He put it into his shirt pocket.

As long as I live I'll believe that Carlos Marcello was sincere when he got down on his knees and prayed for salvation. He didn't have to pretend with me. There was nothing I could do for him except bring him to the Lord.

Unknown to me, Marcello was due in court that afternoon. The government was pressing deportation action against him, in which it never succeeded.

Before I left, he asked me, "If you don't mind, can you come down to the court at two o'clock? You don't have to be seen with me if you don't want to. But if I could just spot you in the crowd, maybe I could think you were praying for me."

I agreed.

When I went outside, there was a battery of television cameramen and newspaper photographers. They were waiting to get shots of Marcello leaving his house.

The courtroom was jammed with reporters. Some of them had come from as far away as Chicago to cover Marcello's deportation hearing. In the midst of all this, I didn't see Marcello as a defendant in court, but as a new creature in Christ. I could see a bulge against the upper part of his jacket. The Bible I had given him was still there. The judge and reporters would have been shocked if they had known that Marcello was carrying a New Testament.

After hearing brief testimony from both sides, the judge postponed the hearing. On his way out, Marcello stopped and shook hands with me. "Thank you, preacher, for helping me find the Lord," he said.

I rushed back to church and excitedly told Dr. Grey of Marcello's conversion. He was incredulous. "I want to talk to him," Dr. Grey said. "I've denounced him a couple of times from the pulpit. I'd like to see if he's really saved."

I phoned Marcello and invited him to dinner with Dr. Grey and myself. A few days later the three of us met at a French Quarter restaurant.

Dr. Grey and Marcello began a long conversation about the prevalence of gambling and prostitution in New Orleans and how much influence the underworld really had in the city.

I interrupted impatiently. "Dr. Grey, ask him if he meant it when he got saved the other day."

Marcello volunteered the answer. "Yes, I did. Otherwise, I wouldn't have done it. In fact, I wouldn't be sitting here right now with you two preachers if I hadn't meant it."

"Then you can thank the Lord for Bob Harrington," Dr. Grey said. "He'll go where angels fear to tread."

"I just wish he, or someone like him, had come to me twenty years ago," Marcello said.

Marcello and I became good friends. He would call me frequently and ask me to join him for breakfast at five-thirty in the morning. None of his servants were awake at that hour, so he'd prepare the eggs and coffee himself. At one of our breakfast meetings, he said, "Bob, don't tell the public too much about what I've done. I'm proud of it, but people might think I'm using religion as a last resort to prevent my deportation."

I told him I'd like him to give his testimony at a small church in Bogalusa, where I had preached several times.

"All right," he answered, "but don't tell anybody I'm coming. Just let it be us and the folks in the church."

We drove up in his Cadillac and as we arrived at the church it was apparent that somehow word had spread that Marcello was coming. Throngs of people were standing outside. There were even people up in the trees looking down as Marcello and I got out of the car.

The local pastor came up to me, drew me to one side, and said testily, "You're going to ruin my church, bringing this man up here to testify."

I told him, "Who is supposed to testify? We're forgetting the name of the game. We forget sometimes that we're supposed to be saving sinners."

I went inside with Marcello and we sat on the platform near the pulpit. The largest crowd in the history of the church was on hand. The pews were filled to capacity and two extra rows of folding chairs had been set up in the rear.

Marcello whispered to me, "Bob, you do the talking. I don't know how to express myself when it comes to religion."

I got up and told the story of Marcello's conversion. I presented him with a small red-covered Bible with his name in gold on the front cover. Then I asked the congregation how many would pray for "the man without a country but a mansion in glory" and practically every person in the church raised his hand.

Marcello, after the show of hands, looked around with an expression of pleasure on his face. He got up and briefly thanked the congregation, saying this was the first time in his life he had been in a Baptist church.

After the service, the members flocked around him, shaking his hand and wishing him well.

The next day, the Bogalusa *Daily News* bannered the story: CARLOS MARCELLO "WITNESS FOR THE LORD." It was the first time I'd seen a headline for God.

"It was an evangelical service the likes of which the church has not seen before," the paper said. "It was a night the members of the congregation will long remember."

7

THE CHAPLAIN
OF BOURBON STREET

I would like to add a happy ending to the story of Carlos
Marcello's conversion. I would like to report that he's out
every day preaching and doing the Lord's work. Unfortunately, I can report none of these things. But even so, for my
part, converting Marcello wasn't a stunt or a grandstand play.
There are only two kinds of people in the world—the lost
and the saved. Marcello was lost when I went to him and he
came meekly to the Lord. In my mind at least, the verdict is
not yet in on whether he will achieve final salvation.

There were several positive things that flowed from my
relationship with Marcello. The news that I had saved him
spread quickly through the French Quarter underground.
Magically, opposition to my presence on Bourbon Street
virtually disappeared. The Quarter was thrown wide open for
me and now I was accepted almost everywhere I went.

Marcello voluntarily began to contribute small sums to my
work. But, more important, his influence helped stabilize my
ministry. Among the denizens of the Quarter, I was no longer
considered a stranger or an outsider. In a sense, I was one of
them, ready to share their problems and help them in any
way I could.

And because of Marcello, I also found a church.

My new church had no pews, stained-glass windows, Bibles or a statue of Jesus. It had no pulpit or room for a Sunday School.

My church was the stage of the Sho-Bar nightclub, where for years the featured attraction had been a stripper named Rita Alexander who casually sipped champagne from a glass balanced on her naked breast.

The club is managed by Marcello's brother Pete, a bespectacled, gray-haired, soft-spoken man in his early fifties.

"What if I convert all your strippers, Pete?" I asked him once.

"The next day I'll have ten to replace each one I lose," he said with high good humor.

The Sho-Bar at least has the reputation of being the best-run strip joint in the Quarter. Sightseeing buses each night bring in a flock of tourists who are chaperoned by a guide. The liquor (for those who want or think they want a shot) is unwatered and girls are not allowed to mingle with the patrons to hustle drinks or their bodies.

Pete invited me to use his club to preach each Sunday afternoon between three and four o'clock. This is still my Bourbon Street "church"—and every Sunday I'm in town I bring the good news of Jesus to my congregation of strippers, club owners, barkers, bartenders, homosexuals, lesbians, drug addicts and alcoholics. Patti White, billed as the "school-teacher who turned stripper," has appeared on stage with me frequently, singing an inspiring version of "What a Friend We Have in Jesus." After one performance, Patti told me, "I'm more nervous singing that song than I am taking off my clothes." I intend to claim her for the Lord once she sees the barrenness of the life she's leading.

At the cost of several thousand dollars, Pete Marcello

changed the interior of his club by moving the bar to a circumspect corner away from the stage where I preach. He has put no restrictions on what I can say or do during my Sunday sermons. I'm also working hard to convert Pete—and it wouldn't surprise me if one day the Marcello brothers both hailed Jesus as their eternal Savior. A preacher, after all, has to be a practicing optimist. I've met thousands of men and women along Bourbon Street who live their lives in the deepest degradation. Yet not one of them is beyond the saving power of God. I believe this with all my heart and soul and spirit, and enough converts have come to me from the pit of total despair to reassure me constantly that my evangelical message pays dividends among the downtrodden.

My Sunday sermons at the Sho-Bar have become a New Orleans tradition. Often the audience is sprinkled with tourists, who consider it one of the "in" things to do while visiting the city. Many of them are saved, too.

Pete Marcello has even erected a small plaque outside the club, which proudly informs passers-by that the Sho-Bar is the "Home of Brother Bob Harrington, Preacher of the Gospel."

On a typical Sunday before my service, the regular barker for the Sho-Bar gives way to my secretary, Sally Stallings, and my two young associates, Ken Hoots and Tommy Winders, who with their clear young voices invite the strolling crowds inside to hear my sermon.

Those who enter are white and black, shoeshine boys and club entrepreneurs smoking two-dollar cigars, strippers and secretaries, tired prostitutes and matrons in sensible shoes. It's a polyglot, ever-changing assemblage—and the people I enjoy preaching to most.

Frequent "Amens," "You tell them, preacher," and "The Lord's a Mighty Force" punctuate my message of salvation. An uncounted number of sinners have been saved on the premises of the Sho-Bar, and they have lived to cherish the day they came—by accident or design—to Bourbon Street to hear a simple Baptist preacher declare the unchanging virtues of old-time religion.

Of course, there has been criticism leveled at me for delivering the Lord's word from an unabashed skin mill. After one of my sermons, a lady who said she was from Tennessee came up and shook her finger in my face. "You are making a mockery of God," she shouted, "and I'm praying for you to die."

I know I've also offended sedate Baptist ministers and some of New Orleans' so-called finest citizens. They are well-meaning people who only feel comfortable in a high-steeple, few-people church where Christ is revered in a "sacred" atmosphere.

But Dr. Grey understands my methods.

"If any criticism can be leveled against Bob Harrington, it would be confined to his approach," Dr. Grey told a reporter. "I believe in him and his spiritual dedication to his work. He and his wife and two children are faithful members of our church.

"You take the average one of us 'first-churchy' preachers— why, the first time we encountered some of that stuff that Bob sees every day on Bourbon Street, we'd tuck in our tails and run.

"I wouldn't be at all in favor of trying to get his ministry to be a church-supported thing, or to make it a chapel with a beautiful ceiling. Those people are not going to come to a place like that to hear preaching; they want somebody to go down there and mix it up and get in there and talk their language and Bob does just that, in a rather dynamic, flamboyant way."

On Bourbon Street I think of myself as a truant officer for Jesus, out catching Christians playing hooky. There are a lot of people running away from God that come down to the skin mills. But we sometimes forget that Jesus saved only sinners. Not once do we read of Him saving a person who was already a Christian. Look at the people who followed Christ in the beginning. Was Saul on his way back from a Brotherhood meeting? Was Mary Magdalene out collecting contributions for missionaries? The employees in the Quarter accept me because they know I'm not trying to close the places down. Sinners admire somebody who stands for something good.

I never take a collection after my Sho-Bar sermons. A lot of people are waiting for me either to make a misstep or to put in a commercial gimmick. The minute it appears my preaching is a money-making venture, my work would be dead on Bourbon Street.

Speaking of money, I remember one drunk who came up to me after listening to my hour-long sermon. I hadn't reached him at all. "Preacher," he asked, "you got a quarter for me to buy a bottle of beer?"

Once I felt secure on Bourbon Street, I decided to leave the seminary and my post with Dr. Grey to devote full time to my work in the Quarter.

My feeling of acceptance in the Quarter, however, was soon shattered by my landlord. He sent me a formal notice of eviction. I had two weeks to pack up and leave my Salvation Shop. When I phoned him and asked why I had to vacate, he explained, "Nothing personal, preacher. But I haven't been able to rent space on either side of your location since you moved in." A beauty shop, which catered almost solely to strippers, had opened on one side of me, but quickly went out of business.

So I had to find new headquarters. Luckily, I located a run-down, unrented building at 225½ Bourbon Street (which is still my address). It was situated between the Blue Angel Club and a saloon, and directly across the street from the Sho-Bar.

I rented it at once, and this time the landlord showed no reluctance. He probably didn't think I'd last long anyway.

My new location wasn't an inspiring sight when I first moved in. There was a long French courtyard leading to a flight of steps and a narrow walkway which bordered a group of neglected, beat-up rooms. None of the walls were painted, the floorboards were rotting and there were rusty iron bars on the windows. The place had once been used to house slaves before they were auctioned off to cotton farmers.

Over a period of time, I had raised more than five thousand dollars from contributions offered at revivals and I used part of Joyce's small salary to put the new headquarters in shape.

There is probably no other mission station in the world quite like it. Only a thin wall separates my display room from the Blue Angel bar. To the left of the top step, a flimsy pan-eled door hides the strippers who work at the Blue Angel from the gaze of my visitors. Beneath my prayer room are the dressing rooms of the strippers. In the alley below, winos scavenge the garbage cans looking hopefully for a bottle with a few drops of booze.

The atmosphere around me is a stench in the nostrils of God. But it's where the action is. Too many preachers sit in air-conditioned comfort in sanctum sanctorums and wait for people to come to them to find salvation. These preachers should put shoe leather in their salvation; they need more holy boldness.

Formal church attendance continues to decline throughout

the United States. And much of the fault lies with the churches. There are not enough activists in any denomination willing to confront sin head-on, or clergymen willing to soil their manicured hands by helping the lost and friendless.

Shortly after opening my new headquarters, I recall, I was walking out of my office late one night. A man with no legs, a local character, was in the gutter. The cripple was drunk, but he recognized me. "Help me, preacher," he pleaded.

I picked him up and put him in a taxicab. A crowd of tourists had gathered and began laughing. Someone shouted, "There's that crazy preacher." Then they started throwing coins at me. I wasn't too proud to pick up every penny, nickel and dime from the sidewalk. The money, tossed at me as a cruel joke, I gave to the wretched man, whose clothes were ragged and stained with vomit.

Then I turned on the crowd and gave them a tongue-lashing. I asked how many believed in Christ. I dared them to step forward and proclaim themselves as Christians who had acted in the spirit of God. Slowly, the crowd broke up. What had been a moment of heartless amusement turned into shame. One woman pressed a twenty-dollar bill into my hand —which I also gave to the legless man.

Indifference, cruelty, lack of compassion for the weak must be dealt with at the source. When the tourists come to Bourbon Street, they're ready to frolic. Anything goes. They leave their morals in the hotel room. They think nothing of running through their bankrolls, yet on Sunday mornings in church their contributions are parsimonious.

On Bourbon Street, I'm blessed with the opportunity to minister to the sick. The well have no need of me.

One night, Bible in hand, I strolled by one of the Quarter's honky-tonks. A prostitute stopped me in front of the bar and said, "Hey there, preacher boy, you lay that book down and we can make some pretty music together."

I just shoved the Bible under her nose and asked her if she was saved. And that was that.

With a thousand dollars worth of financing from a group of religious-minded laymen, I bought a huge billboard, lighted at night, on the corner of Canal and Royal streets in the heart of the business district. "MAY I HELP YOU?" the sign asked in huge letters and underneath was my address and telephone number.

A lot of phone calls to city hall and letters to the editors of the newspapers flooded in, complaining about the billboard. I was accused of profaning and cheapening the Lord.

But I wondered why people objected to advertising God. The daily press and television are filled with noxious ads for such things as deodorants, cigarettes, wine, toilet-bowl cleaners and brassieres.

Doesn't the message of God rate at least equal time and space?

I would rather have an interview in *Playboy* magazine or a billboard in the commercial center of New Orleans than a thousand stories about me and my work in the religious pages of newspapers. That's the way to spread the gospel among those who need it most. In how many American homes is a chapter of the Bible read every day? Is the Bible approached with the same excitement as a college boy's monthly perusal of *Playboy?*

Pornography is a two-billion-dollar business in the United States. How many Bibles would two-billion-dollars buy?

The times cry for men of God to speak their piece before sinners. The social upheaval in America, brought about by the lessening influence of the established churches and family life, has reached catastrophic proportions.

New Orleans advertises itself as the Paris of America. Sin-drenched Bourbon Street is the first place the city's millions of tourists want to see.

Now when they come down to Bourbon Street, they also see something they never expected—a sanctuary of God jammed into a street of a modern-day Sodom.

I glory in the fact that God has made me a witness on Bourbon Street—and I don't intend to disappoint Him.

Word of my ministry had spread faster than I thought possible, and one night in October 1962 I was invited to appear on a radio discussion program with Victor H. Schiro, the mayor of New Orleans. I was flattered that he had heard about my work and that he whole-heartedly approved. On the air he announced, to my surprise, that he was going to issue an official proclamation in my honor.

A few days later I went to the mayor's office and received from him a scroll which said:

WHEREAS, deep and abiding faith and reverence, and an intense desire to help his fellow man have always epitomized his efforts; and

WHEREAS, he has coupled his dedication with bound-less energy, working endless hours in His cause; and

WHEREAS, he has channeled his efforts into those areas not always reached and sometimes overlooked by others:

NOW, THEREFORE, I, Victor H. Schiro, Mayor of the City of New Orleans, do hereby proclaim that Evangelist Bob Harrington be henceforth known as

THE CHAPLAIN OF BOURBON STREET

and I admonish all citizens to take cognizance thereof, and to offer felicitations to this auspicious occasion.

It was one of the proudest moments of my life, and I gloried in my new-found recognition as CHAPLAIN OF BOURBON STREET. I had won my battle star.

I knew I had come a long way since my conversion in Sweet Water less than four years before. But I also knew that my work on Bourbon Street was only beginning.

8

"WHERE THERE AIN'T NO TEN COMMANDMENTS"*

Come with me for a stroll along Bourbon Street on a typical night. This is my parish, and this is the way it is.

By 9 P.M. the street is a seething mass of humanity, choked with pleasure-seekers roaming restlessly down the narrow corridor where every sin in creation can be had for a price.

Ninety per cent of the well-dressed, affluent crowd is composed of tourists, out for a night of artificial thrills.

As I leave my office, a drunk weaves unsteadily on the sidewalk. I recognize him immediately. He's a deacon at a well-known Baptist church in Mississippi where I have preached often. I latch on to him and guide him to a parked police car. He recognizes me, too. But there is no shame in his voice as he declares: "Preacher, you sure have ruined my night."

I stop to buy a hot dog from one of the vendors stationed at every corner. In their candy-striped jackets, the Lucky Dog vendors add a note of quaintness to the street. Their lot is not to be envied—they net three dollars on a good night for eleven hours of work. Most of them couldn't get by on

* From *Mandalay*, by Rudyard Kipling

their pitiful earnings without the help of the Baptist Rescue Mission on Magazine Street.

"How's that boy of yours doing at college, Rick?"

He hands me my hot dog and his face breaks into a smile. "Straight A average," he says. "He isn't going to wind up like his old man."

Rick has a larger income than the other vendors and he's able to support his son in college because of a lucrative sideline: selling dope.

I walk into a spaghetti house for a cup of coffee. The proprietor gives me a somber greeting. Carmen is an unhappy man since his wife ran out on him and became a French Quarter prostitute. He knows that I've come to tell him for perhaps the hundredth time that he must give himself to Jesus in order to lift his burden.

"Chaplain," he says, "you and I have seen how this street destroys people. Anybody who comes down here ought to be shocked into living right when he sees what goes on."

"But when are you going to be shocked into Christian living?" I ask.

"I just don't know, I just don't know," he says moodily and turns away.

Outside again. Next door to the restaurant is a lingerie shop, its windows filled with dirty and suggestive cardboard signs ("French Ticklers" and "Our Birth Control Pills Are 100% Pregnant-Proof"). Those are apt souvenirs for the pornographic-minded. The shop boasts a sale on "Do It Yourself Strip Kits." G-strings, pasties, breakaway gowns, peek-a-boo brassieres, see-through blouses, skirts slit to the hip and panties with red fingers encircling the crotch are among the items for purchase. "We deliver anywhere," a note in the window says.

I move on. In front of every honky-tonk the barkers are

luring passers-by inside. The barkers are a colorful crew, and
they are among my favorite people. I know every one of
them in the Quarter. Unfortunately, many of them are
drunks. The owners of the clubs they work for don't help.
When the crowds the barker steers through the door are
good, a waitress is sent out with a shot as a reward.

Spying me, a barker named Chico chants, "This show is
recommended by the *Ladies Home Journal,* the PTA and
the Chaplain of Bourbon Street."

"Sure I recommend it," I answer as I stop. "I recommend
it to send you straight to hell."

Chico and I are old friends and the repartee between us
is a familiar routine. Though he professes no church relationship, Chico respects my work. One night when a couple of
teen-aged hoodlums tried to vandalize my office, he chased
them off.

At the next joint there's another barker I've known for
years. Dave, an ex-Sunday School teacher who drifted away
from the church, is a tall, lanky Negro. In his spare time, he's
a militant civil rights advocate.

"How's business, Dave?"

"I don't know what's wrong, Chaplain. I can't seem to get
them in tonight."

I listen as he reels off his spiel to a group of three couples in
tuxedoes and evening gowns. Dave's pitch is unconvincing
and lackluster. The couples shuffle on.

"I think I know your problem, Dave. You've lost confidence
in yourself. You've got to expect people to come in and in-
dicate your self-confidence in the way you speak."

"You mean I've got to think positively?"

"That's right."

Dave tries again as another group approaches. This time
his voice brims with assurance. He claps his hands and flashes

a winning smile. "Welcome to the club with the best food and entertainment in all of New Orleans. You won't find more joy anyplace this side of heaven. But to tell you the truth, if you folks don't come in I'll lose my job."

The group laughs—and they pile inside as Dave happily holds the door open.

"You'd make a powerful preacher," I tell Dave.

"See you Sunday at the Sho-Bar, and maybe I'll give my testimony," Dave promises. "And, Chaplain, thanks."

As I continue on, the crowd is thickening. Business on the street is booming. Couples holding beer cans in their hands giggle hysterically, jostling me as they brush by. Sprinkled among the crowd are obvious homosexuals, walking hand in hand. Lesbians, arms around each other's waists, cruise by brazenly.

Outside another joint a sad-eyed wife tugs at her husband's arm, trying to restrain him from entering. The barker is holding the door open and a stripper in the last stage of undress is undulating on the bar. The man shakes loose from his wife's grip and goes in. Helpless, she follows him through the door.

Also in the stream of traffic now are couples holding the hands of five- and six-year-old children. (If minors weren't forbidden to enter their premises, some of the club owners would gladly serve those kids a drink.)

I reach a seedy shop where a group of college boys are gathered around a battery of hand-cranked slide machines that exhibit some of the street's better-known strippers as they peel off their clothes. In a rear room of this establishment, sixteen-millimeter stag movies are shown for a one-dollar admission charge.

I pass a bar with a sign that says: "The only place where intellectuals can discuss politics and broads, philosophy and broads, sports and broads, music and broads, other people's broads, and just broads." I take a look inside. The place is jammed.

My next stop is a coffee shop where strippers congregate between shows. A shapely girl of eighteen named Linda shakes my hand and welcomes me with a big grin.

I tell her, "I've been in your club the last few nights and I didn't see you around. I missed you."

"Glad you did. I've been home sick."

"You mean you've been back in Virginia?"

"Hell, no. I really would be sick if I had to put up with my old man and lady for three days. Preacher, this French Quarter is home to me."

I give her one of my tracts and challenge her: "You're afraid to find real contentment. That's why you won't trust Jesus as your Savior."

"Oh, you know I've tried that. But it doesn't work."

"Not by itself. When Christianity leaves the head to take in the heart, then it works."

Linda shrugs, but she puts the tract into her purse. As I leave her, I pray that she'll read it and be touched by the simple message of salvation it offers.

"I'm only drinking beer tonight, Chaplain," says Johnny, a 260-pound Irish barker, as I approach him. "I can hold my liquor. I can quit anytime I want."

"Then why don't you?"

"I guess it's just habit, but I sure don't approve of these minors getting liquor." Just then a young blond girl comes up and hands Johnny her identification card.

He doesn't even bother to inspect it. "If you're eighteen, my nine-year-old must be twenty-five."

"Are you calling me a liar?"

"If you want to put it that way."

"I'll have you know they just don't give these I.D. cards away."

"No, they don't. They sell them for two dollars right around the corner."

The girl leaves in a rage.

"See what I mean, Chaplain. These youngsters shouldn't be drinking. They ought to put a curb on it."

"They ought to curb their mothers and fathers," I say. "They're the ones who set the example. The kids are only aping what they see their parents doing at home."

I ramble along and spot a wino in a doorway, apparently sleeping off his latest drunk. I bend down and look at him. I know the man. He's a former light-heavyweight boxer who earned more than a million dollars in a fifteen-year career in the ring. At one time, he ranked second only to the champion. An injury to his brain left him punch-drunk. He had visited me at my office on several occasions, but his mind was too dazed and befuddled to comprehend the message of Christ. Broke and friendless, he drifted through the Quarter, drinking and talking to himself. My first thought is to wake him and give him enough money for a room. I bend down and shake him. No response. I put my face close to his. There is no sound of breathing. I place my hand on his heart. There is no beat. I walk to a phone booth and call an ambulance. Fifteen minutes later it rolls up and a doctor steps out. A quick examination. The man is dead. I get down on my knees and say a prayer. I have to fight to keep the tears from coming.

The atmosphere changes dramatically as I reach Preservation Hall, the famous old building where authentic New Orleans jazz is still improvised by a sextet of talented, aging Negroes. At the door, I greet Dolly, a quiet, pretty, dark-haired girl in her twenties wearing a poncho and sandals. I leave several dozen of my gospel tracts with her and she promises to pass them out. She waves me inside.

The music is pure and ricochets off the ancient unpainted walls. As I enter, the jazzmen segue into an inspired rendition of "When the Saints Go Marching In."

After the number, the leader asks me to say a few words. I tell the patrons about my work on Bourbon Street and add: "When it comes time for the saints to go marching in, I hope everybody here tonight will really be in their number."

I'm on the street again. On a busy corner three teen-agers are panhandling. One of them, a girl no more than sixteen, stops me and asks: "Would you like to contribute something so we can get to Los Angeles?"

Her accent sounds local. "Are you from New Orleans?"

"Yes, but we're running away from home. We want to live on the Sunset Strip."

"I'm making a trip to heaven," I reply. "Would you like to hear how you can go along?"

"My heaven is turning on with pot," says the girl.

"Why not turn on with Jesus? He'll give your life purpose and meaning. With Christ in your heart, you'll have nothing to run away from."

The girl looks at me through unseeing eyes. She isn't interested in salvation. But she's young. Hopefully, the moment will come for her when Christ will touch her life.

I use the garbage-strewn back alley to visit the club where Al Pierce works as a cook. Al is a graduate of an Alabama prison. After serving seven years for armed robbery, he was paroled into my custody. I converted Al and got him his job on the street.

"An old cell-mate looked me up today," Al begins.

"You know you have to watch the company you keep."

"Right, preacher. He wanted me to come in on a heist."

"What did you tell him?"

"Told him I'm doing fine right where I am."

"Keep it that way, Al."

"I will. I've been happy ever since you got me right with the Lord."

I push open the kitchen door for a view of the action in the club. Three go-go girls are dancing onstage as psychedelic lights—green, red and purple—sweep the room.

Carol, a fading thirtyish B-girl in a short skirt and revealing sequined blouse puts her arm around me and whispers confidentially: "I need bus fare to Philadelphia. My mother's dying of cancer."

I tell her to come to my office in the morning with her suitcase packed and I'll put her on the bus.

"Forget it," Carol says.

"Why?"

"My mother isn't sick. She died years ago. I just figured you were good for a touch."

I had guessed as much.

Before I can talk to her about Jesus, a customer comes over and offers to buy her a drink. Carol winks at me and wiggles away.

Once more I'm in the stream of traffic. An elderly man in a business suit comes up. "Where can I get a young girl, the younger the better."

"How about coming over to my office and saying a prayer with me?"

"A prayer? What for?"

"To save your sinful soul."

"All I'm interested in is a young girl."

"I'm a preacher, not a pimp."

"Sorry," he says, his eyes avoiding mine. He melts quickly into the passing throng.

The sights and sounds of the street engulf me.

The crowds are becoming unruly, more boisterous.

On the sidewalk outside the Sho-Bar, a stripper is cursing a blue funk. She's angry at the police, who have towed her car away for parking in a restricted zone. Pete Marcello listens stoically.

Bursts of jazz, much of it phony and commercialized, lance the air.

The barkers, their voices pitched high, promise impossible delights.

A thousand, five thousand, acts of infidelity will be committed tonight.

An uncounted number of drinks will trickle down the throats of men to dull their senses and tranquilize their consciences so they can push the reality of tomorrow from their minds.

More than one hundred thousand dollars will be spent this evening along the street for the privilege of watching a hundred bored strippers methodically remove their flimsy costumes.

The lost, the tired, the hopeless, the desperate and the damned are frittering away the hours of their meaningless lives.

It is a world of total unreality.

For a moment, I feel doubt, a one-eyed man in the kingdom of the blind.

Not a single soul has been led to the Lord tonight.

My reverie is broken by a shout of "Chaplain, Chaplain, over here!" I turn and see one of the patrol cars that cruises the Quarter. The police know me—I carry one of the department's few honorary badges.

"Get in, Chaplain," says the officer. "You may be able to

help on this one. Just got a call—there's a girl standing on the ledge of a hotel, ten stories up."

As the siren sounds and we speed ahead, there is dread in my heart. I'm all too familiar with the hotel. So far this month, five people have plunged from its windows and roof to their deaths.

More than two hundred of the morbidly curious are already gathered on the street in front of the hotel. All eyes are looking up at a frail figure who bends and weaves on a precarious perch. A sudden gust of wind would topple the girl into eternity.

I race for the elevator.

Two plainclothesmen are at the window trying to convince the girl to come back into the safety of the room.

So far, their efforts have failed. "Chaplain," says one of the detectives, "you talk to her."

I look out the window. The girl is fifteen feet away.

"I'm a minister," I tell her. "I'm not going to say that if you jump you'll be committing a sin against God. You know that."

"I don't want to talk to you."

"Will you do me one favor before you jump?"

The girl doesn't answer. I climb out on the ledge, praying it is strong enough to hold my weight. I inch closer to her.

"Not another step," she commands.

"I only want to give you this."

For the first time, there seems to be a flicker of interest, an awareness of something outside herself.

"Take my Bible. Hold it. Jump with it if you want to, but take it."

"No."

"Why not? If you're not afraid of death, why be afraid to touch the Book?"

"It's a trick."

"You won't find any tricks in the Bible. But you will find the answer to your problem, whatever it is."

"I'm pregnant," she says. "And my boyfriend ran out on me."

"Then forget about yourself. Think of the baby. Why kill your child without giving him a chance to live?"

I've moved to within a few feet of the girl. "Hold on to the Bible. I'll take you back inside and we can talk."

I wait for a long agonizing moment while she makes the crucial decision. Finally, her hand reaches out. Together, we edge our way carefully back into the room.

"I'm sorry," the girl says.

Five minutes later, I've led her to the Lord.

The girl tells me she'll have the baby, then give it up for adoption.

She walks out of the room, head held high, between the two detectives.

There is strength and courage in her now. And I will do all in my power to reinforce her resolution in the trying months to come while she waits for the baby.

The crowd has dispersed by the time I reach the sidewalk outside the hotel.

It has been a long night.

I walk to the garage where my car is parked. I feel exhilarated on the drive home.

Then the thought occurs to me—tomorrow night Bourbon Street will come alive again.

It will be another typical night, filled with life and death, pain, victory, defeat—and hope.

And I'll be there, carrying my Bible, with Jesus walking at my side.

9

PLEASURE FOR A SEASON

Prostitution in New Orleans is two hundred and fifty years old.

It arrived shortly after the founding of the city in 1718 by Jean Baptiste le Moyne, Sieur de Bienville, the governor of the French colony of Louisiana.

Bienville built *Nouvelle-Orléans* (named for the French Regent, the Duke of Orléans) along a crescent-shaped bend of the mighty Mississippi. With the help of twenty-five convicts and a handful of carpenters, he cleared the forests and alligator-infested swamps and constructed the first crude shacks and barracks.

That accomplished, Bienville implored Paris: "Send me women for my men. They are running into the woods after Indian girls."

Paris responded by culling its prisons and brothels of prostitutes to provide female companionship for the new settlers. Such were the first women (the practical French also sent along a midwife) to arrive in the city.

In 1721, architect Adrien de Pauger laid out the plans for the French Quarter. Soon the prostitutes claimed the Quarter for their own, and under four succeeding flags—French, Spanish, American, Confederate and again American—the area acquired world-wide notoriety as a center for flesh peddling.

By the end of the nineteeth century, New Orleans was inundated by white, black, yellow, brown and red prostitutes.

The Creole whores became a legend. So did the octoroons and quadroons descended from Negro slaves and their white masters.

Lulu White, a West Indian octoroon, was described as "the Queen of the Demi-Monde. She is noted as the handsomest octoroon in America and aside from her beauty she possesses the largest collection of diamonds, pearls and other rare gems in this part of the country."

Early in this century came the invasion of famous madams, who established the most elegant bawdyhouses in the nation.

There was Lulu White's Mahogany Hall, where musical entertainment was provided by such pioneer practitioners of jazz as Louis Armstrong and Jelly Roll Morton. There was also Mae Tuckerman's Mansion, Josie Arlington and her House of All Nations, the Palace, the Anne, the Studio and dozens of others.

From the whorehouses, the term "Blue Book" became part of our language. Each year, the prostitution parlors printed a small blue book with intimate descriptions of their most prominent girls. It was probably the most blatant piece of pornography ever published—giving the vital statistics of the girls, their special talents, photographs, plus phone numbers and the address of the house where each girl plied her trade.

Under pressure from the U. S. Navy, prostitution was finally, though reluctantly, declared illegal in New Orleans in 1917. The law doomed the red-light district, but served only to drive the girls underground.

Today, prostitution still is one of the major evils of the French Quarter.

There is hardly a stripper on Bourbon Street who cannot be bought for the night. Sometimes their pimps are the barkers. And the majority of club owners, despite a law against mingling, introduce their strippers to customers. They find clients for the girls who work for them, and take half the fee.

There is also a hard core of professionals and a weekend invasion of amateurs (secretaries, salesgirls and students) who find prostitution a handy way to supplement their incomes.

A rigid class system rules in the world of the prostitute. At the top are the mistresses, many of them retired strippers, who are ensconced in lavish apartments in the Quarter by their well-heeled benefactors.

A rung below are the $100-a-night call girls, who operate out of equally lavish apartments.

Then, in declining order of prestige and price, are the strippers, the B-girls, the streetwalkers and the amateurs.

As a group, the girls who sell their bodies are a troubled, insecure lot, desperately clinging to their youth by every stratagem known to modern plastic surgery and cosmetology.

Many, under my prodding, have come to the Lord gratefully; others, particularly the younger ones, are more difficult to convert. Nancy is a good example. She was eighteen when I met her under the most disgusting circumstances.

Passing an alley off Bourbon Street late one evening, I saw two shadowy forms silhouetted in the moonlight. I walked toward them, but they were oblivious to my arrival. A girl was on her knees before a half-undressed sailor. After the sailor cried out his satisfaction, the girl rose and saw me for the first time.

Her voice was hard. "I should charge you for watching," she said. "You some kind of pervert?"

"I've just witnessed all the perversion I can stand."

"Tell you what, I'll take you on next for ten dollars."

"Sin," I quoted, "brings pleasure for a season, then it bites like a poisonous adder."

"You sound like a preacher." She moved closer to me. "You are a preacher. I've seen you walking around the Quarter. You're the crazy bastard who wears red all the time."

"I also carry a red Bible. Do you want me to read what the Book says about whores?"

"I'm not really a whore. I'm only doing this to save enough money so my boyfriend can open a restaurant. I've got seven thousand dollars in the bank already. We're going to be married in a couple of months."

"Does your boyfriend know what you're doing to earn the money?"

"Who do you think finds most of my customers?"

"You'll never have a happy marriage with what you've got on your conscience. You need the Lord and you have to change your life—now, at this moment."

"I know what I'm doing and I don't need any smart-aleck preacher telling me I'm a sinner."

I gave her my card and invited her to visit me at my office the next day.

She laughed and started to walk away. "I'll be there. Why not? But it will still cost you ten dollars. Preachers are human, too."

She turned and the sheepish sailor, who'd been too embarrassed to say a word, meekly followed her out of the alley.

Smartly dressed and full of ginger and sass, the girl showed up at my office the next day.

She told me her name and something of her background. She had been in the Quarter for two years, after leaving a home in Baltimore dominated by a drunken father.

"Our family existed on welfare checks. I got tired of all that and decided to make my own way."

"But you chose the wrong way," I said.

"Remember, it takes two to make a bargain. Most of my customers are supposed to be respectable citizens, but they come to me to cheat on their wives."

"Have you had any religious training?"

"You won't believe this—but I sang in the choir."

"Why did you leave the church?"

"I'll tell you the truth. My mother used to get my father sobered up every Sunday morning and we'd all go to services. Then one day—I was about fourteen at the time—my father raped me. Two hours before, he'd said a dozen 'Hail Marys.'"

"Have you thought about changing your life? Christ can help you."

"I don't want to change. The money's too easy. Do you know, I have one guy who calls me on the telephone and talks to me for a half hour. That's all. Just talks to me. Then he sends me a check for fifty dollars every week. You'd faint if I told you his name. He's a real big shot in town."

"The Lord will deal with him. Why don't you let the Lord deal with you, here and now."

"No chance."

"If you aren't interested in God, why did you bother to visit me?"

"Curiosity."

"About what?"

"I wanted to see if you'd make a pass at me."

"Suppose I did?"

"I . . . I would be disappointed."

"Then you didn't mean it when you said you'd take me on for ten dollars."

"I was trying to shock you."

"You shocked me all right. You don't belong in an alley

with a sailor. You belong in the bright world of God's sun-light."

"Preacher, I'm flattered. You're the only one I've ever met who seems to give a damn about me. I don't even think my boyfriend really loves me. I'm just a meal ticket to him."

"Let's try an experiment. Why don't you come to work for me for a couple of weeks?"

"What would I do?"

"You can give my secretary a hand. You can type and file and help me to save sinners. That way, you'd also be helping yourself."

"You'd do that for me?"

"You can start right away."

For the next two weeks, Nancy put in a nine-to-five day in my office. Slowly, her attitude began to change. She was seeing less of her boyfriend and instead of spending her nights entertaining customers she walked all over the Quar-ter with me. She began to see Bourbon Street in a new light.

Then Nancy suddenly disappeared for three days. I was worried—afraid she might have reverted to her former habits.

She turned up unexpectedly one day while I was medi-tating in our prayer room.

My fears proved groundless. Nancy's face was radiant, her eyes shining. There was an air of crisp confidence about her.

Nancy told me she had left town to think things through. She had now made several firm decisions. She was giving up prostitution and leaving her boyfriend. She had been to con-fession and decided to return to the Catholic Church. She was going to finish high school and then study nursing.

I was overjoyed. Nancy had re-entered the human race and discovered the saving power of a deep personal devotion to God. Since that discovery, she has never returned to the Quarter.

Joanna was a different problem entirely. I met her one night while riding in a patrol car with two vice squad detectives who'd been tipped that an orgy was taking place in a Bourbon Street apartment.

I've seen enough in my parish not to shock easily, but what I saw as I entered that apartment was appalling.

There was an attractive girl, dressed only in garter belt, fish-net stockings and high heels, lying on the bed. Five men, a couple of them with cameras, were also in the room. All the men were stark naked.

They were promptly booked for engaging in prostitution and lewd behavior. I went to the jail and put up the bail money for the girl. Then I took her home.

Joanna casually told me about herself. She was from a middle-class family in Iowa, had been divorced a few years before and had come to New Orleans to earn a living. She had been denied custody of her two children because her husband proved in court that she was an unfit, promiscuous mother.

"How," I asked her, "could you indulge in such behavior?"

"Simple. I'm a nymphomaniac. I've had this thing for men ever since I can remember. I can't help it."

"There's only one way to curb the things of the flesh. And that's by concentrating on the things of the spirit."

"If you're talking about God, don't bother."

"Do you want help?"

"Deep down, I suppose I do. But I've tried religion and I've tried psychiatry. The psychiatrist ended up by propositioning me."

"You'll get a better shake from God."

"No sermon is going to change me."

"I'm not going to preach to you. All I ask is that you pray with me, say a simple prayer asking forgiveness and asking

Christ to come into your heart. All you have to do is believe in Him, and your life will change."

I didn't wait for her to answer, but bowed my head and said the prayer. When I looked up, she was staring at me with beseeching eyes.

"You really believe in that mumbo jumbo, don't you?"

"I've given my life in service to God. Prayer is not mumbo jumbo. It's only an appeal for help to someone mightier than all of us."

"What the hell, let me try it."

I repeated the prayer, and Joanna this time joined me in asking for strength to begin a new life.

I left her after extracting a promise that she would stop seeing men. But I knew she needed practical as well as spiritual support. So I called her husband. He told me, despite everything, that he was still in love with Nancy and he agreed to come to New Orleans.

He arrived with the two children and we went to see Joanna. The sight of her children was overwhelming. She broke down and cried. Then she asked her husband, "Please, please, take me home."

I remarried them in a quiet ceremony. I also arranged to have the charges against Joanna dropped.

I still hear from Joanna, now living in a large metropolitan city on the East Coast. She's completely devoted to her family and hasn't broken her marital bond once. Religion is an important part of her life—and not only on Sunday mornings. She participates actively in church work throughout the week. Her "nymphomania" turned out to be an illusion and an indulgence. She found she could be happy with one man. Where she lives now, no one knows, and no one will ever know what she was before she was brought to Christ.

It's been my experience that converting prostitutes is not

difficult if you can infuse two missing elements into their lives: an awareness of the Lord and a new commitment to career or marriage. Once they find spiritual help and the confidence that they can succeed in some endeavor away from Bourbon Street, their transformation is often miraculous. I have found this to be true in case after case.

"Let's face it," a thirty-year-old honey-blond stripper named Sheilah told me one night after her show, "a girl just can't make the kind of money in 'straight' business that a man can. So there has to be a way to equalize things. I wouldn't just crawl into the sack with anybody who came along and waved a fifty-dollar bill in my face. But if a guy is nice and I like him, I don't mind going to bed with him."

"But what are you going to do when you lose your figure?" I asked her. "At best, you've got a few more years and then you'll be washed up as a stripper."

Sheilah shook her head and didn't answer my question. She was determined not to face reality.

It took me a year to win Sheilah to the Lord. The inspiration came one night when she mentioned in passing that she designed all the gowns she wore in her act.

"My wife has a birthday coming up," I told her, "and I want you to create something special for her. But make sure it's a dress that's a little more conservative than a stripper's outfit."

Delighted, Sheilah agreed.

I took Joyce down to Sheilah's apartment in the Quarter for her first fitting.

Sheilah and Joyce became good friends. When the dress was finished, it was beautiful. Joyce often wears it to church Sunday mornings.

Joyce recommended Sheilah to several of her friends. Soon the girl found herself swamped with orders. She no longer had to strip or indulge in occasional acts of prostitution. She had found her "equalizer."

I had proved to her that she could earn money honestly and without the taint of sin.

Today Sheilah owns and runs one of the most successful dress businesses in New Orleans. She's also a fervent Christian and lives her new faith every day of her life.

Though I have converted an uncounted number of prostitutes, I do not mean to give the impression that I have single-handedly banished the world's oldest profession from the Quarter.

Tonight, tomorrow night, and the night after that, the immemorial bargain will be struck between a girl willing to sell her body and a man willing to pay for it.

But the small success I've had with these lost girls convinces me that progress can be made toward eventually driving this illicit traffic from Bourbon Street.

Laws banning prostitution do not work. It is moral fervor and spiritual benediction tied to a pragmatic program of rehabilitation that does the job.

No prostitute is hopeless. No prostitute is beyond salvation.

If I could find a minister, a priest and a rabbi to each take one girl under his wing, prostitution in New Orleans would disappear.

What a glorious thing it would be if there were a thousand Chaplains of Bourbon Street. God needs more than one witness in the French Quarter.

Until that happens, prostitution—and all the other evils of the Quarter—will continue to flourish.

10

THE STRIPPERS

Names like Blaze Starr, Candy Barr, Lili St. Cyr and Patti White are better known on Bourbon Street than the names of Matthew, Mark, Luke and John.

The famous strippers are the idols of the thousands of girls who pour into the Quarter each year from every state in the union.

Their backgrounds are an astonishing cross-section of American society.

I've met a stripper who spent three years in a convent. Another came from the poshest finishing school in Massachusetts. Some are ex-showgirls from Las Vegas, some are winners of the most prestigious beauty contests in America. Others are former schoolteachers, housewives, mothers, divorcees, girls from poverty-stricken backwater towns with grade-school educations and young women with college degrees, products of respectable middle-class suburban families.

There is no "typical" stripper. They have only two things in common—a weak moral code and a lack of faith in God.

Once they arrive on Bourbon Street, the competition among them is ferocious—fresh, beautiful young bodies vying for the opportunity to take their clothes off in front of sex-hungry men.

The most alluring of them are snapped up by the club

owners and given a quick lesson or two in how to shed their clothes provocatively. Then they are pushed onstage to titillate the passions of customers.

I'm frequently asked why these girls become strippers. After talking to hundreds of them, I've determined there are three basic reasons.

Some consider stripping a springboard to a Hollywood contract and fame. They know that Marilyn Monroe made it big after she posed in the nude for a calendar. And Jayne Mansfield didn't become a star by virtue of her acting ability, but by exposing her lush curves in gowns cut to her navel. They point to the increasing nudity in movies, which is accepted, if not demanded, by audiences. These girls know what they are doing is wrong, but they figure they can get by with it until a talent scout discovers them. Stripping is merely a means to an end.

Then there are the girls who are rebelling against parents or unfaithful husbands. They want to prove to their families that they can succeed at something on their own. One girl told me: "Every time I strip I think of my ex-husband. I'll show him that if he doesn't want my body, other men do."

The third group considers stripping as just another job. Usually untrained for any other type of work, they rationalize that they are merely earning a living, much like a girl who labors as a secretary or a dental assistant, and what they do isn't hurting or harming anybody.

But what none of these girls realize is that Bourbon Street is the end, not the beginning, of the road. They soon fall prey to the corruption of the atmosphere—hustling customers for drinks, prostitution, drug addiction, lesbianism, posing for pornographic photographs and performing unspeakable acts of perversion in stag movies.

The neophyte stripper doesn't always take easily to the business.

"I was a hula dancer in a club in Honolulu and the manager convinced me one day that I could make more money if I would do the same act, only take off my top," a stripper billed as Miss Hawaii told me.

"What was it like that first time?" I asked her.

"I didn't even finish the act—I ran off crying. I wasn't going to do it any more, but the manager said I should feel the same way about it as I did in the other act. It's what you feel in your mind—you don't have to want to tease, you can want to just entertain."

"You get used to it," another stripper told me. "I just look past the bald heads and think of something else."

And another girl said: "It gives me a kick, all those men looking at me. They all believe I'm stripping just for them and they dream of having me. You want to know what I think about while I'm up there taking it off? I think: Look all you want, fellows, because you're square if you have to pay to look and that's the only way you could ever see me or be with me. And after a while stripping becomes like nothing."

But some girls never get used to it. Many drink themselves into near oblivion before they summon up the brass to perform. Others get high on marijuana. There are even some who've told me they pray, asking the Lord for courage!

Thanks to the strippers, the Bourbon Street economy booms every night. The girls are the indispensable lure. If they all magically disappeared, the street would be a parking lot.

The law only bars a stripper from sitting down or touching any part of her body while she takes off her clothes. Otherwise, she can gyrate, shake, wiggle, bump, grind, tell off-color jokes and bring her body to within inches of customers, who urge her on while shouting obscenities.

"I tried to legitimatize my act, give it some dignity," Linda Brigette, one of the street's best-known strippers told me. "But the public wouldn't accept it. On Bourbon Street, they want it dirty, dirty as possible."

The average stripper peels down to her G-string in less than five minutes. They work three or four shows a night, about a total of twenty minutes. For their brief labors, salaries begin at seventy-five dollars a week and range up to more than five hundred a week when they become headline attractions. Some of the girls double and triple their income by prostitution.

As far as I know, I'm the only man permitted free access to the backstage dressing rooms of the strippers. No questions are asked as I carry my Bible into the drab, unglamorous quarters where the girls wile their time away between shows playing checkers, writing letters home or reading movie fan magazines.

Striding through a club one evening while a stripper named Monica was performing her notoriously torrid dance, I saw the girl suddenly collapse onstage.

I helped carry her backstage and called a doctor.

"It's appendicitis," the doctor told the girl after an examination. "You need an operation and the sooner the better."

I never expected Monica's reaction. "But that would leave a scar. No guy wants to look at a big, red, ugly scar on a girl's belly."

"If you don't have the operation," the doctor added with finality, "you'll be risking your life."

"If I can't strip, I won't have much of a life worth saving."

So enmeshed had Monica become with her career as a

stripper that she was apparently willing to gamble her immortal soul for the dubious rewards of her profession.

Over the next few weeks, I counseled every night with Monica, urging her as forcefully as I could to submit to the operation.

But she was unmovable. The doctor had frozen the inflamed area around the appendix and Monica was performing again. "That doctor," she said, "had me scared for a while. But what does he know? I feel fine."

I checked with the doctor, who told me, "The freezing process is only temporary. She can't keep going much longer without the operation."

Though I continued to plead and beg, Monica flippantly disregarded me. If she was worried at all, she didn't show it outwardly. But I suspected that inwardly she was terrified.

As a last resort, I talked to the owner of her club, explained the situation, and tried to get him to fire her. "Won't do any good, preacher, she'd only get a job someplace else on the street."

I prayed for Monica, but the Lord chose another course for her. She was found dead in her apartment by a roommate little more than a month after the doctor's diagnosis.

What a needless, senseless tragedy. A beautiful girl dead at twenty-three, a useless sacrifice for a job in a cheap skin mill. A routine operation would have saved her. Had she accepted Christianity, she could have gone on to a useful life as a wife and mother. God had given her ample warning and a clear sign she was destined to leave Bourbon Street. The girl chose to ignore not only the Lord, but common sense.

Monica, in the full flower of her beauty, left Bourbon Street in a hearse. She had performed before thousands and been applauded lustily in her brief career.

But there were only three mourners when I conducted her funeral service.

Tragedy lurks everywhere for the Bourbon Street stripper. Having excited the passions of liquor-sodden customers, she is the natural target of men seeking to fulfill their sexual fantasies.

I met Wanda as a result of a small story that appeared in the morning paper. According to the account, the twenty-one-year-old stripper had been beaten and raped by two unidentified men. Wanda had accepted a ride home offered by the two men in a restaurant where she was having breakfast after her last show.

The men, instead of driving her home, had cruised around the city, found a lonely spot, then attacked her. She had a severe bruise over her right eye, two broken ribs and a mild concussion.

I went to the hospital and Wanda greeted me warmly. "I've come to win you for Christ," I told her at the outset. "By now you must realize the life you're leading is taking you straight to hell."

Wanda began confiding in me with childlike eagerness. She was raised, with six brothers and sisters, on a farm in North Dakota. A high-school dropout, she couldn't abide the thought of spending her life in a small rural community, ending up like her mother marrying a farmer and raising a flock of kids. She wanted a touch of glamour and excitement in her life. Blessed with an appealing figure, she had worked as a barmaid in Chicago, a movie cashier in Minneapolis and a dance instructor in several cities. Then she drifted to New Orleans and in exchange for a night in bed with a club owner she had been given a job as a stripper.

But there was more to the story.

Wanda told me that she was three months pregnant. She

admitted that since her arrival on Bourbon Street she had slept with more men than she could remember. She had no idea who had fathered her baby.

But she knew one thing with certainty. The "glamour" and "excitement" of life on her own had worn thin. Raised as an Episcopalian, Wanda was ready to renew her faith in the Lord.

"I need something in my life, preacher. I feel empty and afraid."

I kneeled at the side of her hospital bed and helped her for the first time in her life to have a truly personal confrontation with Christ.

Subsequently she had her baby, a healthy eight-pound boy, but Wanda refused to give her child up for adoption. After the baby was born, she returned to North Dakota and married her childhood sweetheart. She is a farm wife now and the mother of two more children. She had her fling at the world of phony excitement and unnatural thrills. Today she is content and at peace with herself.

I treasure a line from one of her letters: "Finding the Lord was the most important thing that ever happened to me."

I have discovered that there isn't a stripper on Bourbon Street who doesn't need spiritual help. And my ministry among them has been unusually successful, once they come to the realization that they are pursuing precarious, short-lived, sin-drenched careers.

"I've had it with this Godforsaken street," a stripper named Joan told me when she paid an unexpected visit to my office.

"I woke up this morning and found some guy standing over me and my pasties were off and so was my G-string. I remember going to bed with them on. For all I know, the guy had intercourse with me while I was sleeping and I never woke up. It sounds crazy, but I sleep like the dead."

I listened incredulously to Joan's bizarre story, then asked her if she was ready to accept the saving power of Christ.

She took the Bible from my desk and hugged it to her breast. "Once I believed every word in this Book," she said, "and I want to believe it all again."

Joan, it turned out, had studied comparative religion at a university. She was an extremely intelligent, sensitive girl who had strayed from the church.

"I wish I had been born ugly," she told me. "Having curves in all the right places is a curse. Most of the men I've met are like animals. All they want is to paw you and go to bed. You wouldn't believe some of the offers I've had. Perverts who wanted me to beat them, whip them, chain them. I don't want to be a prostitute, I've got to get out of New Orleans."

She came to the Lord in a spirit of renewed conviction. After leaving New Orleans, she continued her education, received her Ph.D. in psychology and is now a clinical psychologist in Alabama. Her fee is twenty-five dollars an hour, and, from the well of her own experience and the degradation she suffered while she was on Bourbon Street, she is in a unique position to help her troubled patients. Unlike that of the run of modern psychologists and psychiatrists, Joan's therapy is closely related to God.

With clocklike regularity, I receive each month from Joan an unsolicited check for a hundred dollars. Financially and spiritually, she is one of the most avid supporters of my work.

The strippers of Bourbon Street and most of the club owners have come to look upon me as a friend. Consequently, I'm often the first one called when an emergency arises.

Such an emergency occurred late one evening when my office door flew open and a highly agitated, florid-faced club owner came rushing in.

"Preacher, I've got big trouble," he said.

"They catch you selling drinks to teen-agers again?"

"No, nothing like that. It's Diane, my star attraction. She's locked herself in her dressing room and won't come out. I've got two hundred people in my place who've paid to see her. Maybe you could talk to her."

"You've come to the wrong man. I won't ask the girl to strip. My job is to save her from that."

"If you don't come, I'll have to call the cops."

Sensing a soul in trouble, I followed the club owner to his honky-tonk, located a few doors down the street.

The dressing room area was in bedlam when I arrived. Strippers, barmaids and assorted hangers-on were milling around, some of them shouting and pleading with the girl to come out. I cleared them all away. Then I scribbled a quick note on my card and slipped it under the door.

In a moment the lock turned and through a small crack came the defiant, suspicious voice of Diane.

"What do you want?"

"Let's talk," I said.

She opened the door and I walked in.

"Your boss tells me you don't want to go out there and take your clothes off. Congratulations."

"Congratulations nothing," she said angrily. "I want to do my act. I'm ready to do my act, but I can't work this show." Her eyes dropped to the floor and her voice softened.

"Why not?"

"I'm ashamed to tell you."

"Then I'll take you home."

"I don't want to go home. If I walk out of here, I could lose my job. Maybe I've already lost it."

"I'd count it as a victory for God if you never stepped foot on that stage again."

"I don't want to hear any crap about religion."

"Someday you'll be sorry you said that. Meantime, I want to help you if I can. You can't stay locked up in here and you won't go out on the stage."

Diane took a deep breath. She was a magnificently endowed girl in her early twenties wearing a clinging green sequined sheath.

"Do you honestly want to help me?"

"Any way I can."

Diane thought it over, and then unburdened herself. "There's a man sitting at the bar. I spotted him after my last show when I went out to have a drink with a friend. I can't face that man."

"What makes him different?"

"He's . . . he's my father!"

"At least that proves there's an ounce of shame left in you."

"Look, preacher. I make a damn good living as a stripper. I'm not cut out to be a nun. I like my work. Just do me one favor, get my old man the hell out of the club. He's the one with red hair and horn-rimmed glasses sitting at the end of the bar."

"On one condition. Give me your word that you'll come to my office at noon tomorrow and face your father."

"What good would that do? He hates me, and he always has."

"Maybe we can turn that hate around and find love."

"All right, but just get him out of here."

I walked to the bar and introduced myself to Diane's father. I had already decided, difficult as it might be, to tell him the truth. He took the news without visible shock.

"At least we know where she is. Her mother and I haven't heard a word from her since she ran away two years ago. I never thought I'd find her in a place like this."

"She never thought she'd find *you* in a place like this."

He put down his drink, paid his check and left the club with me. Waiting for a taxi back to his hotel, he said, "I'm a businessman in Shreveport. Here for a convention. I can't understand that daughter of mine. We gave her everything."

"Diane's coming to my office tomorrow. I think it would be a good idea if you were there, too."

He readily agreed.

The next day, Diane, her father and I got down to business. There were no embraces between father and daughter when they saw each other. They sat at opposite ends of my desk, both of them obviously uncomfortable.

"Diane," I said, "you told me yesterday you thought your father hated you."

"It's true. He was never around when I needed him and he never forgave me for not being born a boy so I could follow in his footsteps as a businessman."

"You're wrong, Diane," the father said gently. "I gave as much love as I could. And now I'd give my life if I could convince you to come home. Your mother has never gotten over the pain of your leaving."

"I like Bourbon Street," Diane answered. "I intend to stay here."

"If you do," the father said with sudden firmness, "I'll be at that place every night watching you take your clothes off."

Diane sighed. She knew she was beaten.

"Let's compromise," I said. "Diane, why don't you go home with your father? Try it for six months. See if you can patch things up. The Bible tells us to banish hate from our hearts. With love, all things are possible."

I took them into the prayer room and called on God to bind the wounds of a daughter and father who had grown apart through a terrible series of misunderstandings.

At the conclusion of my prayer, both Diane and her father were weeping.

"I know," I said, "it's going to be difficult for both of you. But you've made a start. Through God comes understanding and true devotion."

I gave them each a New Testament and they walked out arm in arm.

Their reconciliation wasn't easy, according to Diane's first letters. The pain was too deep for a pat solution. But gradually the hatred between Diane and her father was dissipated. The girl also developed a more meaningful relationship with her mother. And she came to understand that she had worked as a stripper only to punish her father.

Nowadays my letters from Diane are postmarked from South America. She's serving with the Peace Corps as a medical technician.

Her life, thank the Lord, has been redirected. For Diane, Bourbon Street now is only a bad dream.

Unfortunately, hundreds of other Dianes are still living their bad dreams on Bourbon Street.

But there is always hope.

Peggy's nightmare ended on the day she voluntarily came to me for help. Originally from New York City, Peggy was eighteen and had been a stripper for only a year. In that short time she had become a favorite on the street because of the uniqueness of her act. She performed with tassels tied to her pasties, exhibiting remarkable muscular control, which made her a quick star and a sure crowd-pleaser. But the disintegration of her personality had come with bewildering speed.

Here, word for word, is the conversation between Peggy and myself that led to her conversion.

"Why did you come to New Orleans?"

"I had a boyfriend in school at Baton Rouge and I thought if I lived here we could be together."

"How did you become a stripper?"

"When I was in New York I was a go-go girl for about two years. I started here as a go-go. But I wasn't making enough money. So I dreamed up this gimmick of twirling tassels. I don't know why, but the guys went wild."

"How much money do you earn?"

"Three hundred dollars a week."

"When you first started, were you nervous walking out on the stage?"

"No. I had worked topless when I was a go-go girl. I was used to the idea that my bust was showing."

"Weren't you at all embarrassed?"

"Yes, a little."

"Does your family know what you're doing?"

"My mother does. She's the only one. My father's dead. If he was still alive, I probably wouldn't have become a stripper. But my mother doesn't look at it as doing something sleazy or something bad. She just thinks it's a part of show business."

"Has your mother seen your act?"

"She hasn't seen me strip, but she saw me when I was a go-go dancer."

"And she didn't object to your dancing topless?"

"No."

"What's your religious background?"

"Lutheran. I went to confirmation and Sunday School when I was a kid."

"When was the last time you were in church?"

"Three, four years ago. I'm not sure."

"Do you see any relationship between being a stripper and leaving your religion?"

"I didn't in the beginning. I felt that I could strip and still keep myself respectable. But then things started happening fast."

"Such as?"

"I got this sudden fear that, if I kept sleeping with my boyfriend, I would become pregnant and couldn't work any more. So I stopped seeing him. Then one night a girl I work with propositioned me."

"She wanted you to commit an unnatural act?"

"She was a lesbian. But she was so nice and so beautiful, I tried it with her. I really enjoyed it—at first."

"Did you begin feeling guilty?"

"Yes. But I really broke it off because the girl got too possessive. She was more jealous of me than a man."

"Did you go back to your boyfriend?"

"I tried, but he wouldn't have anything to do with me. That made me mad. So I started working stags, private parties in hotel rooms or somebody's apartment. I got two hundred dollars every time I did it."

"Didn't that disgust you?"

"No. It was the same as working in the club. But I stopped stripping at those parties."

"Why?"

"I was gang-raped. They tied my hands to the bed and six or seven men forced themselves on me."

"Did you report it to the police?"

"What good would it do?"

"Did you tell the owner of your club what had happened?"

"Sure. He laughed."

"Are you pregnant?"

"No."

"Did you continue stripping after that?"

"Only in the club."

"And you still didn't feel there was a place in your life for God?"

"In a way. Somebody told me he had used LSD and seen heaven."

"Did you try it?"

"Yes."

"What kind of a trip did you have?"

"Bad. Very bad. I remember crawling through this cave on my hands and knees. People were staring down from the walls at me. They were all wearing masks, layer on layer of masks. It was horrible. When they finally took the last mask off, there was Snow White and the Seven Dwarfs."

"How did you feel when the drug wore off?"

"Depressed. Like committing suicide."

"I hope you didn't try that."

"No. I went back to work and stayed away from the drugs."

"Do you know that the Bible says your body is the Temple of God?"

"I remember reading that."

"And yet you've violated your body."

"That's the only way a girl can make out on Bourbon Street."

"Why did you come to see me?"

"I read one of your pamphlets. It was tacked to the dressing room mirror of a girl who works with me."

"Did the pamphlet help you?"

"It said that God offers forgiveness. I've been an awful sinner. Can He forgive me?"

"Yes."

There it was, Peggy's story as she told it matter-of-factly, freely and without dramatics. If there was ever a soul in torment, it was Peggy's. Not yet out of her teens, she had tasted the seamiest side of life on Bourbon Street. Her year in the Quarter had been one of unrelenting self-indulgence. She had tried to flee reality, but reality had grimly and inevitably caught up with her.

Peggy and I prayed together and she came to the Lord gratefully. To buttress her faith I outlined a course of religious instruction that would keep her strong and resolute.

Joyce, Rhonda, Mitzi and I had a farewell party for Peggy. She was going back home and planned to enroll in business college.

We gave Peggy a few small gifts—a Bible, a silver cross and a picture of Jesus.

Peggy, as she was saying good-by, pressed a package into my hands. I opened it and found that she had given me her tassels—a symbol of her final break with Bourbon Street.

Peggy now is one of the trim, happy, well-adjusted advertising girls who flood New York's Madison Avenue. She has an excellent job that carries a great deal of responsibility.

Her future, because she found Christ in time, is bright and unclouded.

My own faith is restored whenever I think of ex-strippers like Wanda, Joan, Diane, Peggy and others who have made it out of the ghetto of sin that is Bourbon Street.

Their places, of course, have long since been filled in the honky-tonks. Every night the ritual goes on. Garments are flung off and naked flesh exposed.

The strippers are still hard at work on Bourbon Street.
But so is God.

11

FRED MARLOW'S LAST DRINK

Alcohol lubricates Bourbon Street. It is the oil that powers the engines of sin and makes millionaires of the smooth operators who own the honky-tonks.

While he watches a parade of strippers in one of the skin mills, the typical customer consumes three drinks. That's an outlay of six dollars. Figuring an average of five hundred customers a night, the club owner grosses $3,000 daily, $21,000 a week, more than a million dollars a year. Some clubs do less than that amount of business; some, considerably more.

Without the sale of liquor, the cash registers in the honky-tonks would be silent and much of the sin on Bourbon Street would dry up.

But these days it's passé for a minister of the gospel to preach against the evils of drink, though Scripture is very clear on the subject.

Proverbs 20:1: "Wine is a mocker, strong drink *is* raging: and whosoever is deceived thereby is not wise."

Proverbs 23:29–30: "Who hath woe? who hath sorrow? who hath contentions? who hath babbling? who hath wounds without cause? who hath redness of eyes? They that tarry long at the wine; they that go to seek mixed wine."

Isaiah 5:11: "Woe unto them that rise up early in the

morning, that they may follow strong drink; that continue until night, till wine inflame them."

So ancient and familiar a foe is liquor that a sermon against it in a modern church is considered the ultimate in bromides. The churches have thus joined in a conspiracy of indifference to the nation's number-one mental health problem.

Nevertheless, the shocking statistics remain and the immeasurable toll in human suffering caused by drinking cannot be swept away.

There are between four and six million alcoholics in America today and the figure is increasing by 500,000 each year. After heart disease and cancer, alcoholism is our biggest killer. One third of the beds in mental institutions are occupied by alcoholics. Half the annual 50,000 fatalities in automobile accidents are caused by excessive drinking. The ever-burgeoning increase in crime is directly related to the ever-burgeoning increase in the consumption of liquor. Throughout the nation, there are more barmaids serving liquor than there are girls attending college.

Babylon, Sodom, Gomorrah, Greece and Rome were undermined by overindulgence of strong drink.

The same fate threatens America.

One indication of this clear and present danger to our country is the unbelievable fact that the United States government has put its official stamp of approval on drinking! Financed by a $1,100,000 grant from the Department of Health, Education and Welfare, a recent 198-page report issued by The Cooperative Commission on the Study of Alcoholism urged that the legal drinking age be lowered from twenty-one to eighteen, that drinking at cocktail parties and other social gatherings be encouraged and that "drinking should be shown as a type of activity that can add enjoyment to life."

We ignore history, turn our backs on a problem that shatters the lives of millions every year and do not protest when $1,100,000 of the taxpayers' money is used to justify a blatant sin against God.

Isn't it time that it became fashionable again for churchmen to cry out against liquor? As spokesmen for the Lord, only the clergy offer a way out for the alcoholic.

Psychiatrists admit they do not know what causes alcoholism. They treat patients for the affliction but it is a long and expensive process and there is no guarantee of a cure.

The only sure cure is God.

This has been recognized by Alcoholics Anonymous since its formation in 1934. The organization has been most effective in treating alcoholics—it has an 80 per cent recovery rate. In A.A., the alcoholic comes to believe that only a power greater than himself can restore his life, and he turns his will and life over to the care of God as he understands Him. The alcoholic undertakes a searching moral inventory of himself, admits to God and one human being his wrongs and shortcomings and calls on God to remove them. He seeks by prayer and meditation to improve his conscious contract with God, praying for knowledge of his will and the strength to carry it out.

As a former drinker myself, I do not approach the hundreds of alcoholics I minister to each year with a holier-than-thou attitude. But I tell each of them that my personal experience and my work with other hardened alcoholics proves that drinking can be stopped only by finding God.

It is that simple, and that complicated.

Until the alcoholic has a spiritual experience, he will never be freed from the curse of drinking. There are thousands of rehabilitated alcoholics in America who will testify to that.

One of them is Fred Marlow, a thirty-two-year-old plumber

who conquered the bottle after I brought him to Christ. Of all the cases in my files, Fred's rejuvenation best illustrates how the power of the Lord can help even the alcoholic who has hit rock bottom. It's a story of parental disrespect, trouble in school, juvenile delinquency, uncontrolled drinking, narcotics addiction, illicit sex, an attempt at suicide and a stay in a mental hospital.

I worked with Fred for a year, counseling him and strengthening his resolve whenever he was tempted to take a drink. At the end of a year, Fred reached a milestone. He hadn't had a drink in all that time. Fred came to me on the anniversary of his spiritual rebirth and, for the first time, told me the full story of the degradation he had suffered before he was saved. He did so in the hope that his experience would help and inspire other alcoholics.

Seated comfortably in my office, Fred pulled no punches as he responded to my questions.

"Where were you born?" I began.

"Here in New Orleans. I had a hell of a time from the moment I came into the world. According to my father, I was given up for dead when I came out of my mother's womb. I was black and blue and I wasn't breathing. The doctor said saving my life was hopeless, so he handed me to a nurse while he worked on my mother. The nurse took me to a sink, put me under hot water, then cold water, then she spanked me. Finally, I started crying. It was a close call."

"Do you think that experience had an effect on your later development?"

"Possibly. It's shock enough to be born, without the additional shock I had at birth."

"What did your father do?"

"He was a builder, but he never made much money, ninety

to a hundred dollars a month. That was during the Depression."

"And your mother?"

"She was a housewife and a college graduate."

"Did your parents have a good marriage?"

"No. There were always arguments and bickering. It was only in the last five years of my mother's life, while she was dying of cancer, that my parents became close. My mother was bed-ridden and my father did everything he could to make her comfortable. She died three years ago. My father told me he never realized how much he loved my mother until her illness."

"How do you feel about your father?"

"I love him now. But when I was young I resented him because I thought he could have done more for me than he did."

"In what way?"

"Material things. I had to work to buy my bicycle and my clothes. But he never deprived my sister of anything. If she wanted a new dress, he bought it. And when she needed money to go to college, he provided it."

"What was your attitude toward your mother?"

"I took advantage of her. If she wouldn't give me something I wanted, I'd tell her she didn't love me. I worked her like a con artist. Whatever money she had, I could get easily. And I could make her do other things. If I wanted something and she wouldn't give it to me, I told her she didn't love or understand me. That made her feel bad. Then she would go ahead and allow me to have whatever I wanted."

"Did you love her?"

"Not when I was growing up. In fact, I wished she would die. Many times I can remember wishing she was dead."

"Why?"

"Because she showed such a lack of faith and trust in me. She would stand at the door when I got ready to go out and she'd beg me not to get into trouble with the police. Of course, she had reason to feel that way, because I had been brought home once by the police."

"How old were you when that happened?"

"The first time I was in trouble with the police I was twelve. I stole a car. We didn't have a family car and I just wanted to drive around the block."

"Did you go to church as a youngster?"

"Every Sunday morning. If I went to church, I would be allowed to go to the movies in the afternoon. Until I was thirteen or fourteen years old I went to church every Sunday. Then I told my folks I didn't want to go any more—and that was that. I always resented going to church. I didn't like it at all."

"Why not?"

"It was dull and uninspiring. I didn't understand the sermons and the lessons. I thought religion was a lot of bunk and a pack of fairy tales."

"How did you do in school?"

"I could have done much better. I was always in trouble."

"What kind of trouble?"

"Hitting the teachers or throwing things at them."

"Why did you do that?"

"Because they were always telling me to do things I didn't want to do. And then they'd grab me and force me to obey. But whenever they grabbed me, I'd hit them or kick them or pick up a book and throw it. Once, I threw a pair of overshoes at a teacher when I was in first grade. I threw them with all my might and hit her. But the blow didn't knock her down, which is what I wanted to do."

"Why did you throw the overshoes?"

"I'd hit my sister on the playground and the teacher slapped my face."

"For what reason did you hit your sister?"

"Just because I was ornery. I don't remember any other reason."

"You were pretty mean and rebellious as a child."

"That's right, starting at the age of four when I set the house on fire."

"How did that happen?"

"I wanted to smoke, so I rolled up a piece of paper like a cigarette and I sneaked into the laundry room and lit it. The paper burned real fast and it started to scorch my lip. So I threw it in the clothes hamper. The fire started and spread to the kitchen. My uncle was a member of the fire department and when he came to the house he picked me up under one arm and carried me out in front of the fire engine. It was a big diesel and it was roaring and loud. He told me it was a giant red devil and would eat me up if I ever did such a thing again. I believed him and I grew up afraid of diesel engines. When I got into the Navy, I had to work around diesel engines and I was so afraid of them that I got emotional headaches."

"As a youngster, did you run with a gang?"

"Yes. We called ourselves 'The Boys.' We thought we were pretty tough. We had homemade zip guns, chains, lead weights and brass knuckles. We'd cut out sharp points on the brass knuckles, then put a roll of pennies or a solid steel bar in our fist. When you hit somebody with that, it would really tear his face up. One Saturday the word got around that we were going to have a big gang fight after a football game. So the police were there and, out of five hundred kids, they arrested five of us. I was one of the five. The police decided they would make examples of us even though the fight never came off. They kept us in jail over the weekend."

"How did you feel about that, did you resent the police?"

"I've always resented any authority. Father, mother, teachers, police, anyone that could tell me what to do and be able to enforce it."

"Since you disliked going to church, what were the important things in your life when you were young?"

"Sex and drinking."

"Did you receive any sex education from your parents?"

"No. I learned about it on the streets. I had my first girl when I was eleven years old. I really didn't know what was going on. She was showing me and she was younger than I was. I don't remember it being a good or a bad experience, just an experience. The first time I remember enjoying sex was when I was about thirteen; that was the first time I found out there was a lot of satisfaction in it and from that time on I kept getting satisfied. We also had a lot of gangbangs. Seven or eight of us would go to one girl's house and we'd draw straws to see who would be first. The girl would always tell me to be first and the others had to draw the straws. That bolstered my ego."

"What did you think of a girl who would do that?"

"She was a nice girl. I liked her. Emotionally, I was never what you'd call real adult. If there were ten of us in line and I was the eighth guy I would fall in love with the girl and try to talk her out of having relations with the next two. I also remember when I was about fifteen that a bunch of us would ride our motorcycles up into the hills. We'd drink wine and mess around and then we'd have intercourse on the motorcycle. We'd put the kickstand down, start the bike up, gun the engine, place our jackets on the tanks and put the girl on the seat and stretch her out over the tanks."

"How old were you when you had your first drink?"

"Nine or ten. I'd have a glass of beer or maybe a shot of whiskey. I got it from one of my uncles or at the house of one of my buddies. When I was twelve I really began drinking, really started to purposely get drunk."

"Why?"

"I thought it was fun. It was also a way to show off."

"Did you feel good when you were drunk?"

"Very good."

"How much were you drinking at the age of twelve?"

"I wasn't drinking every day because I didn't have the ways to get it. But I would get drunk at least once a week. Then, when I was twelve, I started using marijuana."

"How did that happen?"

"I was with a couple of other kids and they said it would be a big kick. I'd heard about it and I wanted to try it—I was willing to try just about anything. So I tried it and I enjoyed it. I got high and I thought that was awful smart and show-offy. I was big, big-time. It made me a big man instead of a little, tiny shriveled-up kid. It made me feel grown-up whenever I could get drunk or high on marijuana."

"Did you use any other narcotics in your teens?"

"Benzedrine tablets, yellow jackets and red devils. The yellow jackets and red devils are barbiturates, a sleeping compound of some kind. You'd take a lot of bennies with them and you'd get real dopey but you wouldn't go to sleep."

"How long were you on narcotics?"

"From the age of twelve until I was twenty. I was taking marijuana and bennies all that time. I was also drinking, but not too heavily. I didn't need to get drunk on liquor while I was using marijuana and Benzedrine. I don't think I got drunk more than a couple of times in that eight-year period. We felt that was being a lush. Being drunk was beneath us, we thought that the kids who got drunk were stupid. Because we would get high on marijuana and Benzedrine and have control of our senses . . . if you can call them senses. Anyway, we wouldn't pass out like a drunk. We were often sick to our stomachs, but we'd be awake and aware . . . if you can call it awareness."

"How did you shake the narcotics?"

"When I started going with my wife. She didn't approve, so I told her I'd quit. I stopped using narcotics three months after I met her. I was in the Navy at the time and I went to a chaplain. He worked with me and prayed with me for about four hours that first night and then I went to see him several times after that and he tried to help me help myself."

"Did the chaplain bring you to God?"

"No. He was a good, sincere man and talked about how important it was to reach out to a power mightier than myself. I didn't really understand what he meant. What actually made me quit narcotics was that I was aboard ship and the stuff wasn't available. Later, when I was on leave in Tokyo, I went to a brothel and smoked a pipe of opium. I finally gave up narcotics by going back to liquor. It was easier to get. And I began drinking very heavily."

"What kind of service did you see in the Navy?"

"I was in the Korean War for nine months on an amphibious communications ship. We directed landings, we even had an admiral aboard. We were hit by bombs twice and sixteen of the crew were killed. Then the ship struck a mine and put us out of action."

"When did you get married?"

"After I got out of the Navy. But I wasn't ready for marriage, I wasn't emotionally mature. I'm still not mature and I've been married ten years. I don't know if you ever reach maturity, but you've got to develop to a certain point before you get married. It's taking on quite a responsibility, which I wasn't prepared to do. I realize that now. And then, as you have kids come along, you have more responsibility and you even resent that a little bit more."

"Did your wife's parents approve of your marriage to their daughter?"

"Her mother did everything in the world to break us up. She even threatened to get a court order against me if I didn't discontinue seeing her daughter until she turned eighteen. That was for about an eight-month period. We had to sneak around to see each other; I wasn't allowed to come to her house to pick her up and take her on a date."

"Why did her mother object to you?"

"She actually wouldn't have liked any man. It wasn't just me. At the time, I felt it might be, but it wasn't. She didn't want her little girl getting married. She wanted her to stay home and take care of the house and she wanted her to go on to college. Her mother didn't want her to get married— period. Especially not to a non-college graduate or someone who wasn't interested in college. When my wife turned eighteen, her mother said she'd give us an engagement party if we'd wait a year until her daughter completed junior college. But we couldn't wait. We eloped. My father and mother also tried to talk us out of it. But we were both of age and we went against everybody's wishes."

"Did your wife know about your drinking?"

"Oh yes. I was drinking and she drank, too. Not like I did, by any means. She would have one beer to my twenty beers or one highball to my twenty highballs."

"How much were you drinking at that stage?"

"At least a quart of hard booze every day."

"Where did you get the money to buy your liquor?"

"On Bourbon Street. I became a professional con man for a

time, working the shell game and the pigeon drop on the suckers. I also rolled prostitutes. I'd find one and get her drunk. They were alcoholics, unfortunate people, I understand now. I didn't understand at the time. I felt they were just drunken sluts and they deserved to be taken. I used to roll queers, too. I'd hit them on the head and take their money."

"Have you ever felt violent or angry, like you could kill someone?"

"Many, many times."

"Was this when you were drinking?"

"Yes."

"What time of day did you take your first drink?"

"Soon as I got up. I needed that alcohol, my system was crying for it. It was a mental and physical obsession—so much so that I decided to buy a bar."

"That way, you'd have all the liquor you wanted?"

"Right. Also I got big-headed. I wanted to make money and I figured I was extra-smart. I'd build it into a big cocktail lounge with dining and dancing. I was really going to make myself a killing."

"Where did you get the money to buy the bar?"

"From my father. He loaned me ten thousand dollars."

"How long did you have the bar?"

"Seven months."

"Was it successful?"

"No."

"Why not?"

"One reason is I was drinking up the profits. You have to realize that I didn't know at the time that I had a drinking problem. I drank all the time, so I didn't know what it was not to drink. I was twenty-eight years old when I bought the bar. The night of our grand opening I was in a traffic accident.

I was half drunk while I was driving and I pulled up to a stop sign. And a guy doing about forty miles an hour rear-ended me. My wife was in the car and he knocked us clear across the intersection. My wife suffered a herniated disc and her tailbone was damaged. She had to have an operation, she had three inches of her tailbone removed. She was in the hospital forty-two days. We had three children by that time and I had to hire somebody to come into the house and take care of the kids. I had to hire extra help at the bar. The bar wasn't making the kind of money to pay for all that plus what I was drinking. I was drinking probably thirty to forty dollars worth a day. So I had to sell and get out from under the payments."

"What did you do then?"

"I tried suicide. I took eighty sleeping pills, but they didn't work."

"Why did you want to kill yourself?"

"It seemed to me that it would be better for me and for everybody concerned if I was dead. I was having trouble with my wife and I didn't have the money to drink like I wanted to drink. I was working in a factory and I came home at noon one day because a transformer burned out and the plant had to close up until it was repaired. So they sent us home. I was getting laid off the next day anyway and I thought this was a pretty dirty deal that this should happen to me. On my way home I stole a half-gallon of wine from a store, ninety-nine-cent wine. I drank it all. I also drank another fifth of wine we had in the house and a fifth of vodka. Then I drank a six-pack of beer, half a fifth of gin and a quarter of a fifth or more of bourbon, all in a four-hour period. And that's when I took the sleeping pills. I woke up in the mental ward of the hospital. I don't know how they saved my life."

"What kind of physical shape were you in during your stay in the hospital?"

"I was run-down. I was weak, tired and nervous. I ached all over. I was suffering from vitamin deficiency and malnutrition, all the things an alcoholic suffers from. They also found out I had cirrhosis of the liver and my gall bladder was in bad shape. In fact, the doctor said I was sixty-five years old inside. All my organs were double my age because of alcohol and the way I'd lived for twenty years. I had four tumors removed and they built me up physically. But not too well, because I was only in there ten days and they discharged me. The doctor let me out on a Sunday night and I had an appointment to see him the following Tuesday. In the meantime I was to lay around and take it easy. I asked the doctor if I could have a drink and he said I could have *a* drink. So I proceeded to get smashed. I stayed drunk day and night, drinking from six in the morning until two in the morning. Every day I was drinking two quarts of bourbon and a lot of brandy. I drank so hard that when I went back to the doctor on Tuesday he said no more drinking. I said okay, fine, no more drinking. I didn't drink Tuesday, but Wednesday I started again. I drank all the rest of that week, clear into the next week. I was up to three quarts a day. And then I'd go to a bar and have triple shots. Then double shots and after I was fairly well loaded I'd go to singles and I'd just sip on them the rest of the time until two in the morning. In the meantime I went back on Benzedrine tablets, taking nine or ten a day. That's how I could stay awake and drink so much over such a long period of time. I ended up back in the psycho ward. That's where I met Janet. She was an alcoholic, too."

"Did you think you could help each other because you both were alcoholics?"

"No, not at first. It was just a physical attraction. After a period of talking to her and playing cards and games, we decided we needed sex relations. So we had them in the hospital in the middle of the night. There were room checks every hour and when the nurse came around I'd fake sleep. Then I'd go down to Janet's room before the next check. We were together every night, and after we left the hospital we rented an apartment. We both started drinking again. We drank steadily for a week. Then I had to leave town for a couple of days to visit my sister. When I got back, Janet was gone. No note. She just vanished. I couldn't figure out why. It upset me quite a bit. I found out she was living in the Quarter with another guy, an old boyfriend she thought she still loved."

"Do you know why Janet became an alcoholic?"

"She came home one day and found her husband in bed with some fat old bitch. That triggered her. It gave her an excuse to do what she probably had been wanting to do. And she kept drinking because she felt so guilty about the things she was doing. The more she drank, the more guilty she would feel. It's a vicious cycle. This is the pattern that brings you right down to the depths. Actually, you want to punish yourself for the things you've done by doing worse things. It's a real sickness."

"Since you seem to understand why Janet drank, do you understand the reasons for your own drinking?"

"I drank to escape myself."

"Did you find yourself so unworthy?"

"Yes."

"Why?"

"I'm just beginning to understand it. I used to think I was something else, I thought I was really something special. And I couldn't understand why other people didn't realize this. I had a very high opinion of myself consciously, but subconsciously I despised myself for the things I did and the way I was. I thought myself completely incompetent, that I couldn't do anything worthwhile. I guess I have a passive-aggressive personality, which is pretty common for alcoholics. I was either way up in the clouds or completely down in the dumps, like a snake crawling on its belly. There was no middle ground, no happy medium. When I was down I drank because I felt sorry for myself and when I was up I drank because I was so damn happy with myself. So either way I drank. Either to celebrate or to relieve emotional pain. When my feelings were hurt I would drink so that there wouldn't be any more hurt. Then it finally got to the point where I wanted to quit. For two years I went to doctor after doctor, then to a psychiatrist. But nothing worked. Then one day I was walking down Bourbon Street—actually I was looking for a bar—when I saw your sign. I walked in and the way you talked to me was the most beautiful thing I'd ever experienced. You showed me how to give myself to Christ. I was amazed, I never knew that God could make things so easy if you only have faith in Him."

"What's your feeling now about God and religion?"

"I can't put the two together. I don't think religion has a whole lot to do with God. I don't think God, if he returned to earth, would have much to do with religion the way it is. I believe in God with all my heart, but separately from religion. Religion is more like a fraternity. You go to church to show everybody your new car and your new clothes. You listen to the minister. But most people don't seem to pay too much attention to him and the ones who do pay a lot of attention are only getting that minister's viewpoint or that particular denomination's viewpoint. Whether it's right or wrong, I don't know. But it doesn't seem to me that they're teaching you that you have a personal obligation to God."

"What is your conception of God?"

"It's a power, not a person. I can't see a man up in the sky with a long gray beard. God is a way of life, a good way of life. It's a strong power. God could take shape or form, I'm sure, but it's not necessary. His shape or form could be you or me and He works through all of us. I don't know why, but you can turn to this power and He will lead, guide, direct you, help you, lift you up from the depths to the heights, maintain you if you'll let him. And this is what He wants to do. Then you become an instrument of God. And this is how you reach your happiness, this is where happiness is, in finding this place of complete rest because you're in the will of God and doing His will."

"Do you still feel anger in your heart?"

"None."

"Do you hate anyone?"

"No."

"What do you think of yourself now?"

"I'm starting to become a pretty nice guy. But it's a slow process. I'm getting nicer every day—it's surprising."

"How are you getting along with your wife?"

"Very well. We've come to understand each other. I'll never forget what she told me before I went to the hospital the last time. She said, 'If only you'd die, if only you would drop dead.' That's how much she hated me because of what I was doing to her because of my drinking."

"What are you going to do with the rest of your life?"

"I want to help people, someway, somehow, in some shape or form. The only happiness or contentment you receive is by giving it away. It's really a selfish motive, but then again it's a thrilling thing to help somebody else, to do something for somebody else just because you want to, not for any reward, not for anything, just because you want to. You get a kind of satisfaction that can't be obtained in any other way. And that's what they mean when they say happiness comes from within yourself. You're able to give to other people just because you want to. It fills you up. It's a great feeling."

"What place does the Lord hold in your everyday life?"

"I take God by faith. I use my emotions instead of my intellect to understand God. I have faith that this is how God works through you. Not through your mind, because your mind will do nothing but destroy you. In trying to reason things out you go crazy because you can't find the answers. But everything will be given to you if you have faith. God made everything in this world and He made it in such abundance that there's plenty to go around. If people would just stop trying so hard, it would be given to them. There's enough for everybody. You don't have to go out and grab it. Nobody is going to get it all. This doesn't mean that I won't strive and use all my ability in my work. But now I'm going to let God lead me."

"Physically, how do you feel since you've stopped drinking?"

"Great. Your body is a wonderful thing. In another year I can be back almost to normal, because the organs will repair themselves if I continue to keep the alcohol out of my system. Your body was given to you by God; how you use it is up to you. If you use your body and mind in the right way, you're going to be physically and spiritually healthy."

"You've been sober for one year. How can you be sure you won't slide back?"

"Because God is with me every moment of my life. With God I feel strong, sure and confident. Fred Marlow has taken his last drink."

12

A DOPE PUSHER'S PARADISE

It's passed quickly from hand to hand in the dressing rooms of strippers, in dimly lighted corners of the honky-tonks, in alleys, on street corners, in the jazz palaces and in the back of respectable-looking shops.

Marijuana, heroin, morphine, methedrine, bennies, goofballs, LSD, DMT, DET and STP—the entire tragic, mind-dulling array of dangerous drugs is sold every night on Bourbon Street.

The Quarter has become a dope pusher's paradise and the traffic in narcotics has increased in recent years to alarming proportions.

Worse than alcohol in its effects on the mind, body and spirit, narcotics reduce their victims to living zombies. Crime, broken families, decimated bank accounts, insanity, death and the loss of a place in heaven are the cruel rewards of the addict.

Senator Thomas J. Dodd, after a careful study of the narcotics problem in America, gave his congressional colleagues a heart-breaking insight into the problem:

"Drug addiction is one of the most baffling social and emotional diseases known to our society. It is a vicious affliction because it dehumanizes the individual, it takes away one's motivation, it destroys will power, and it turns men and

women into walking corpses moved about by a force beyond
their control.

"So far, in spite of all the efforts put forth, we have failed to
find a cure for this terrible illness. We have failed in psychiatric treatment methods; we have failed in medical treatment methods; and we have failed to eliminate narcotics
addiction through punishment and correctional efforts.

"In our Federal hospitals for drug addicts and in various
state mental institutions and psychiatric clinics experts are
continuously working with hundreds of patients. These scien-
tists have found ways to cure the physiological dependence
on drugs. But they have not devised successful methods to
handle the emotional and psychological conflicts and de-
viancies which drive the potential victims of narcotics to
escape reality, to run away from life, and to seek out the
criminal drug peddler because they cannot face the ups and
downs of everyday living without a 'chemical crutch.'

"Although psychiatrists and psychologists provide various
types of therapy while the addict remains in the hospital, they
have difficulty keeping him there once the physical effects
of excessive drug use are eliminated.

"The addict turns to the city streets again and again to meet
his 'contact' because, although the doctors have cured his
physiological dependence on drugs, they cannot give him the
will power to refrain from repeated addiction. Thus a vicious
cycle begins anew. The addict's desire for the drug is so
strong that he will steal and rob and even kill for it."

Senator Dodd's charges of a direct relationship between
narcotics addiction and crime is documented in the daily
reports of the police who try to keep law and order along
Bourbon Street. As an honorary member of the New Orleans
Police Department, I frequently accompany the officers in
their blue and white prowl cars as they cruise through the

Quarter. I have personally witnessed the following cases involving crimes by narcotics users:

A customer who had been ejected from a bar for creating a disturbance returned fifteen minutes later with a shotgun and fired eleven shots into the crowd. Three people were killed, seven wounded. A number of shotguns, rifles and pistols were found in the man's apartment. A large quantity of marijuana was also discovered. The man admitted smoking marijuana that day and on numerous previous occasions.

Three men were spotted by officers entering an antique shop on Royal Street. They were captured and in their stolen car was found a .38-caliber revolver and a large quantity of heroin. One of the men had been paroled from prison six months earlier and all three were later identified by victims as members of a robbery gang involved in numerous thefts.

At 2 P.M. one morning, a thirty-one-year-old waitress flagged down our car and reported she had been kidnapped and robbed. She said that a man had held a knife at her throat and forced her into his car. The man offered her a marijuana cigarette but she refused. He then took fifty dollars from her purse and shoved her out of the car. When the robber was caught a few days later, police found three bags of marijuana in a closet of his apartment.

A block off Bourbon Street one evening about midnight we saw a parked car with five teen-agers, the youngest of whom was thirteen. When we reached the car the odor of marijuana smoke was apparent. The youngsters all admitted smoking marijuana just prior to stealing the car.

The purse of a seventy-eight-year-old woman was grabbed by a teen-aged boy after he struck her with his fists. She fell to the sidewalk, striking her head, and died of a skull fracture. Witnesses identified the youngster and he was arrested for murder. In his home, twenty capsules of LSD were found.

Although he was only seventeen, he had a record of nineteen prior arrests for narcotics offenses.

We answered a call regarding a disturbance at one of the most fashionable apartment buildings on Bourbon Street. When we arrived, the manager told us that a man had run up the stairs with a bumper jack in his hand and had entered an apartment. We raced upstairs and could hear a woman screaming, "Don't kill me, Frank, please don't kill me." The officers broke the door down and the woman cried, "Oh, God, please come in, he's killing me." A man was standing over the woman with a jack handle in his hand, poised to strike. He was taken into custody and a marijuana cigarette was found in his pocket. The man later confessed that he had smoked four marijuana cigarettes that day.

A landlady in another apartment building reported that one of her women tenants had fired two shots at her. We went to the address and knocked at the apartment door. It was opened by a well-dressed woman in her early thirties. In her hand and pointed directly at us was a .25-caliber automatic pistol. We grappled with her, knocking the gun from her hand. A search of her purse revealed two plastic bags containing marijuana.

"Woman screaming" was the report that flashed over the police car radio on another occasion. When we arrived at the apartment we were met by a man and a woman each claiming to be the victim of an assault by the other. The woman's face was bleeding and there was a bruise over her right eye. The man was on the couch with three knife wounds. "I smoked two or three roaches," the woman declared. "Then I picked up the knife and stabbed him." A search disclosed marijuana debris in several ashtrays.

The chances are good that none of these crimes would have been committed if the participants hadn't been using drugs.

"We have failed to find a cure for this terrible illness," Senator Dodd said.

But there is a cure. The addict must get hooked on God. Christ is the world's most potent stimulant. Unless the confirmed drug user makes a commitment to the Lord, he's completely lost, doomed to a life as a "walking corpse."

A doctor at one of the leading hospitals in New Orleans, who is an admitted atheist, told me that it costs $50,000 to treat one addict. And 95 per cent of those who are treated are never cured. He added with unconcealed amazement, "The only permanent cures we see are those who are converted to Jesus Christ."

My own experience with addicts confirms this. Consider the following men and women who had been given up as hopeless until I brought them to the Lord. All of them are now leading useful, successful and fulfilling lives as Christians. But what pain and anguish they suffered until they were saved.

John Ashton, thirty-one. Addicted to heroin nine years. Maintained a twenty-five-dollar-a-day habit through burglary, shoplifting, bad checks and peddling narcotics. He was in and out of jail in New Orleans four times and spent a year and a half in an Army hospital. He's been off drugs for three and a half years.

Louise Darland, twenty-seven. A heroin addict for ten years. Had a thirty-dollar-a-day habit. Convicted of prostitution and shoplifting. She was in custody at Lexington Federal Hospital on three occasions. She hasn't touched drugs for eighteen months.

Carl Baxter, forty-two. A slave to heroin for fourteen years. Burglary, armed robbery and bad checks provided the means for him to support his twenty-five-dollar-a-day addiction. He was in the local jail twice and served thirty-six months in the Atlanta Penitentiary. Clean for three years and one month.

Mauguerite Jackson, nineteen. Addicted to LSD and morphine for three years. Financed her twenty-five-dollar-a-day compulsion through prostitution, theft and selling narcotics. She was a patient in a private sanitarium on two occasions and in the county hospital six times. She's been free of drugs for three years.

James Lewis, twenty-two. Buckled under to marijuana for two years and heroin three years. He spent approximately twenty dollars a day for drugs, raising the money by burglary. He gave up his dependence on narcotics seven months ago.

Alice Carmichael, thirty-nine. A junkie for nine years. She raised the daily twenty-five dollars a day she needed to buy heroin through prostitution, selling narcotics and working as a cocktail waitress on Bourbon Street. At various periods, she was confined in the county jail, the state mental hospital and Lexington Federal Hospital. No use of drugs for the last three years.

Earl Collins, forty-five. He was wedded to heroin for twelve years and collared the cash for his staggering seventy-five-dollar-a-day addiction by robbery and pimping for his wife. By the time he settled on Bourbon Street, he was a graduate of San Quentin Prison in California, Lexington Federal Hospital (three times) and Bellevue Psychiatric Ward in New York (twice). He gave up drugs two and a half years ago.

Through the miracle of Christ, all these addicts were reborn.

It took another miracle to bring Barry Eliot, a nineteen-year-old unemployed dock worker to the Lord. I first met Barry one night while I was making my rounds on Bourbon Street. Walking past a honky-tonk called the Gunga Den, I saw him stagger out the door and into the street directly in the path of an oncoming car.

I moved quickly, pulling him back to the sidewalk. The car narrowly missed hitting both of us.

Barry collapsed and slumped to the ground—a black-eyed, brown-haired youngster about six feet tall with a tortured expression on his face. He was semi-conscious, vomit staining his clothes and blood oozing from a cut on his jaw.

As I started examining him, a crowd began to form around us. I heard a gray-haired grandmother say to a small boy who was obviously her grandson, "You'd better be good or that's how you'll wind up." A man in a dinner jacket and a woman in an evening gown were laughing as I took my red handkerchief out and began wiping the blood from Barry's jaw. A teen-aged girl in black tights told her boyfriend to snap a picture of the spectacle. "That's the Chaplain of Bourbon Street. I saw him a couple of weeks ago on the 'Art Linkletter Show.'"

I put my Bible under Barry's head. A barfly named Charlotte came up and asked if she could help. I told her to bring a damp cloth. She returned in a few moments with an aluminum pan filled with tap water and a red and white checkered napkin. I doused the cloth in the water, wrung it out, and bathed Barry's face. He seemed to be having a hard time breathing, so I undid the two top buttons of his shirt. I also whispered a prayer.

Barry was mumbling incoherently. The only words I could understand were "Ruby" and "Mother."

I shouldered my way through the crowd and snagged a cab. The driver and I got Barry into the back seat and we sped to Southern Baptist Hospital. When we pulled up to the emergency entrance, two orderlies put Barry on a stretcher.

In the emergency room, Barry slowly began to regain consciousness. His first words were, "I need a fix—quick!"

"You've had your last fix," I told him.

"Drop dead," Barry said. Then he whipped the sheet off, leaped up and began swinging. He hit me in the nose and wrestled with the duty nurse, knocking her glasses off. I grabbed Barry and got him down on the floor after dodging a series of wild punches. I put my full weight on his chest while the nurse held on to his legs.

An orderly came in with two half-inch leather straps. We got Barry to a bed and the orderly snapped one strap across his chest and the other around his legs. Barry struggled with frenzied might against the straps, shouting obscenities all the while. A doctor arrived and gave him a sedative. It calmed him down and in a few moments his eyes seemed to be in focus. He looked at me and asked, "Who are you?"

"Only a preacher who pulled you out of the way of a car about forty-five minutes ago."

"I don't need any preacher's help," Barry said defiantly.

"You've got it, whether you want it or not."

"What are you going to do with me?"

"I'm going to see that you're kept here until you shake the drugs."

"I can go cold turkey if I have to. I've done it before. But no one can keep me from getting the stuff once I'm out of here."

"Satan's got you bound up tighter than a ball of yarn," I told him. "I'm going to help you. You've got to make a vital decision in your life—drugs or decency, lunacy or the Lord."

The orderly rolled Barry out. He was still cursing and straining against the straps.

I went to the business office, signed for Barry, then called Joyce and told her to pray for the boy.

Arriving home after midnight, I had just finished the roast beef sandwich Joyce left for me on the kitchen table when the phone rang. It was the hospital chaplain and he told me that

Barry had escaped. He had talked the night nurse into loosening his chest strap. After she left the room, he threw off the leg strap and fled the hospital.

I was determined to find Barry and save him from himself. But where in the French Quarter could he be? The next day I called Charlotte and she told me he hung out in a dive across the street from Pete Fountain's place.

I knew the dive—it was a gathering place for homosexuals, one of the most notorious joints on the street, catering solely to the Godless gay boys who brazenly display their deviation every night. As I walked in I saw the usual crowd, men paired off, openly kissing and petting at the tables. Some wore their hair long, pretending they were women, with rouge, lipstick, mascara, earrings and pointed fingernails painstakingly manicured.

I asked the bartender what time Barry usually came in. He said he would probably arrive any moment.

I took a seat in the rear. Next to me were a pair of giggling gay boys. I heard one of them utter a curse against God. I jabbed him and he let out a squeal. "May God have mercy on you," I told him. My voice carried throughout the room. Every eye in the place turned toward me. The bartender came over and said to the one who had blasphemed God, "What in the devil is going on? Do you have your girdle on too tight again tonight?"

Laughter broke out. The two perverts got up and left.

I waited about fifteen minutes and then I saw Barry coming through the door. He was holding hands with a man I recognized as one of the richest, most reputable merchants on Canal Street. (His wife had come to me for counseling a few weeks before and complained that her marriage was failing. No wonder!)

Barry and the merchant had a drink, then the businessman kissed Barry and walked out.

I wanted to confront Barry alone, so I didn't approach him at that moment. I watched as he gave the bartender some bills. The bartender then went to the back room, returned shortly and handed Barry a package.

The pattern was beginning to emerge. Barry was supporting his drug habit with money obtained through his homosexual relationship with his wealthy benefactor.

As Barry got up and left, I followed him. Taking long, quick strides he walked a couple of blocks and turned in at a cheap hotel.

I went into the dismal narrow lobby and asked the clerk for the register. Barry's name wasn't listed. Then I remembered that the night before Barry had mumbled the name Ruby. I rechecked the register. The third name down was B. R. (Ruby) Briggs, Room 210.

I bounded up the wooden steps two at a time and threaded my way through the dark hallway. I found the room and knocked. A woman's voice called, "Who is it?"

"Reverend Bob Harrington. I want to talk to Barry."

I could hear Barry's voice through the thin door. "Tell him I don't want to see him."

I shouted, "You'll see me or the police. Take your choice."

"Damn it," Barry said. "Open up, Ruby, and see what he wants."

I was surprised at the neat, tidy room. Red lace curtains lined the two windows and fluffy white throw rugs covered much of the scarred yet clean linoleum floor.

"This is the guy who had me strapped down last night," Barry told Ruby.

"Did you also tell her that I pulled you out of the way of a car that might have killed you."

"I don't believe you did it," Barry said.

"I didn't expect any appreciation," I answered. "You know why I'm really here."

"What *do* you want with Barry," Ruby asked.

"I want him for the Lord," I said.

Ruby looked anxious and nervous. She was petite, auburn-haired and not unattractive. I wondered what she could see in a dope-dazed sinner like Barry.

"How long have you been in New Orleans?" I asked Ruby.

"About three years. I teach the second grade at a local elementary school."

A schoolteacher and a narcotics addict. It seemed the unlikeliest of combinations.

Ruby went on, "I met Barry on Bourbon Street about two months ago. I invited him to stay with me. We're living in a common-law relationship."

"As soon as I can afford the ring, we're going to be married," Barry said. "We'll have a preacher and the whole works."

From the adoring look on Ruby's face, she apparently believed that Barry was completely sincere.

"Barry needs somebody to take care of him," Ruby said. "He had rheumatic fever as a youngster and every night I have to give him a shot for it."

I didn't want to break her heart, but I had to disillusion her.

"You're not giving him shots for rheumatic fever. You're injecting him with heroin."

"What did you say?" Ruby asked with shock in her voice.

"Barry is on dope. He's an addict. I found him unconscious last night on Bourbon Street."

"I don't believe you," she said.

"You can verify it by calling the Southern Baptist Hospital."

Ruby took a look at Barry. He didn't say a word. Then she ran from the room in tears.

"Now look what you've done," Barry said.

"Son, why don't you grow up? That dope you're putting into your body is going to destroy you. I saw you in the bar tonight and I know how you're getting the money to support your habit. There's only one way out for you. You need the Lord. He can save and purge you from the craving for dope. Tell me the truth—if you had a choice, would you want to kick the habit?"

"Sure, but—"

"You're looking for one thing in life—yourself. You're looking for Barry. You've tried to escape him long enough with dope. But it doesn't work, does it? You still haven't found yourself and I don't think you're a happy man."

"Have you ever met a happy man?"

"Thousands of them—all living with God in their hearts. And many of them were worse sinners than you before He forgave them."

"But He wouldn't forgive me."

"Yes He will. He gave His only begotten son to make your forgiveness possible."

"I don't understand."

"I don't either. It beats me how Christ dying on the cross two thousand years ago would have anything to do with the way we live here in the twentieth century. But by faith I've found that what He did back then is real and meaningful right down to this very moment."

"What do I have to do to get the kind of faith you're talking about?"

"Nothing. You only have to accept Him, what He has already done and what He will do if you let Him into your heart. You receive His promise of eternal life as a gift. Just claim it."

Barry decided to give the Lord a try. So did Ruby. I put a

hand on each of their shoulders and led them to the Lord. Barry wept from his heart. Then, after yielding himself to God's Spirit, a smile of satisfaction crossed his face.

He told me that his father had died when he was three years old and while growing up he did everything possible to make his mother's life miserable. He had been on dope for three years, and he was afraid he was going to end up in prison because he eventually would have to turn to burglary to supply himself with the ever-growing amount of money he needed to support his habit.

Barry experienced a glorious conversion and swore off drugs.

And he kept his word.

By sheer will power, buttressed by his new-found faith, he stayed clean.

Two months after his conversion, I was leaving for a week-long Crusade in Missouri. I suggested that Barry accompany me. He was overjoyed.

An overflow crowd of more than nine hundred, many of them teen-agers, turned up the first night of the Crusade. I had Barry give his testimony.

Simply, sincerely, he told the audience he wasn't a public speaker. He said that his knees were shaking so furiously he was afraid he'd collapse any moment.

The audience applauded him, and that seemed to give him strength.

Barry poured his heart out. "I want especially to talk to the young people here tonight," he said. "I want to level with you about life. You don't dig life until you dig yourself and Jesus." He was talking the language of the youngsters and they were listening.

"Rolling joints, smoking pot, shooting heroin isn't life. That's plain dumb. I know because I did it for three years. Now I'm turned on with Christ."

Tears rolled down Barry's cheeks. The crowd was moved. Many in the audience reached for handkerchiefs.

"You teen-agers who are looking for thrills," Barry continued, "stay away from dope. Let the gang call you square. Sure, junk will get you high. It got me so high that I tried to kill myself seven times to get rid of it. If you don't believe me, come up and count the razor scars on my wrists."

Throughout the week, churches and civic groups brought delegations of young people from miles around to hear Barry repeat his testimony. Many of the teen-agers surrendered their lives for full-time Christian commitment as a result of hearing Barry.

Now Barry was truly happy for the first time in his life. He reconciled with his mother and he bought that wedding ring for Ruby. I had the pleasure of marrying them.

That was more than two years ago, and Barry has been free of dope ever since. He and Ruby have a baby now and Barry holds down a good job.

Barry still attends Crusades with me on occasion. He's always eager to give his testimony and he has helped me tremendously in my work with other addicts.

Like so many others before him, Barry found a totally new life in Christ.

Not for a second has he regretted the decision he made for the Lord. Through salvation, his future brims with promise and purpose.

Barry learned the greatest lesson in the world—nothing is impossible with Christ in your heart.

13

MAY I HELP YOU?

The Area Code is 504.

The telephone number is 529-5886.

And thank God for Alexander Graham Bell.

Assisted by my staff, our telephone ministry handles thousands of calls every year from people in despair, on the verge of suicide, lonely people with vague anxieties who call in to hear a healing word about God. Often a simple prayer will bring peace to the heart of a disturbed soul and soothe him into sleep without a Nembutal.

There are other calls, too, many of them unpleasant and bizarre. Drunks, nuts, freaks, unbelievers who telephone to taunt, insult, threaten and utter the foulest curses imaginable.

I've come to expect all kinds.

One night I had a call I'll never forget.

"May I help you?" I asked as I picked up the receiver.

"I'm going to kill myself," a man's voice said. "Do you want to hear my pistol go off on the phone?"

"Think a moment," I answered. "God is the one who gives life and He is the one who takes life."

"There isn't any God." The voice was hoarse and foggy. I could almost smell the alcohol over the wire.

"Have you been drinking?"

"How else do you think I got the courage to do what I'm going to do?"

"Why don't you use some of that courage to stand up for the Lord?"

"The goddamn Lord never did anything for me. My wife's run off with another man. She took the kids, even the silverware, and cleaned out the bank account. I have nothing left."

"You have your almighty soul. You have beauty, pride and dignity. You have the strength to rebuild your life."

"Words . . . words . . . words."

"They're words all right, but there's power in them. Those words represent the fundamental teachings of Jesus."

"I'm going to let you hear the sound of the bullet, preacher. My brains are going to be splattered all over this room."

"Before you pull that trigger, I'd like to tell you one thing."

"What's that?"

"How your tombstone is going to read: 'Here lies a man who missed his chance at heaven.'"

The sound of sobbing followed by a sudden wail came over the line. Then the phone went dead.

Had I reached the man? I wondered if he would take his life. I couldn't get him out of my mind and I thought about the call incessantly.

The next night, when I picked up the ringing phone, I didn't recognize the voice. It was cheerful and controlled. "Remember me?" the caller said. "I phoned last night and told you I was going to kill myself."

"Thank the Lord you're alive."

"I'm ashamed of myself, preacher. I don't know how, but I'm going to work out my problems. I want that place in heaven."

I asked for his name and address and if he wanted to come in for counseling.

"No," he said, "I've got all the faith I need in the Lord. I just lost it for a while last night. But I'm going to be all right."

I often think of that man and how his life was spared because he had a number to dial for help.

One day, a long-distance call came in from a lady in New Jersey. She sounded hesitant and apologetic.

"Before I ask a favor, I should tell you I'm Jewish."

"Do you believe in God?"

"Of course."

"That's all the bond two strangers need to help each other."

"I'm so glad you look at things in that light, Reverend. I'm calling about my daughter. I know she's in the French Quarter and we're terribly worried about her. She's been gone for two months. Do you think you could find her?"

"I'll try."

The distraught mother gave me a detailed description of her daughter, and I set out to look for the girl. Luckily, I found her at the third bar I visited. Martha told me that she had applied all along the street for a job as a go-go girl, but had been turned down everywhere.

"How fortunate you are," I said.

I told her about the call from her mother. Her eyes brightened. She admitted Bourbon Street had been a disappointment. Now she was filled with fear and longed to see her parents again.

We went back to my office. I dialed her mother, and there was a tearful, joyous reconciliation on the phone. The next day Martha was happily on her way back to New Jersey.

The telephone encourages candor and anonymity. It is a beacon in the night for the lost.

Late one evening I heard the soft, gentle voice of a man.

"I won't tell you my name, preacher. I saw the doctor

today. He was honest with me. He said I only have a short time to live. I'm seventy-two years old and I've had a good life. But I've had no time for Jesus and I don't know the Bible as I should. I would appreciate it if you could read something from the Book that would comfort me."

The man was obviously sincere, and I felt a lump rising in my throat.

"Do you have a Bible in your home?"

"I'm ashamed to say that I haven't."

"I would like to meet with you personally, and bring you to the Lord."

"No, preacher, I don't think I'd care to do that. I'm not afraid of death, I just want to die quietly without troubling anybody. But I would like to hear some words from the Bible."

"Then mark this down. It's from the Book of John, Chapter Three, verses sixteen through eighteen."

As reverently as I could, I read the passages to him:

"For God so loved the world, that he gave his only begotten Son, that whosoever believeth in him should not perish, but have everlasting life.

"For God sent not his Son into the world to condemn the world; but that the world through him might be saved.

"He that believeth on him is not condemned: but he that believeth not is condemned already, because he hath not believed in the name of the only begotten Son of God."

"Thank you, preacher," the man said, and hung up.

I never heard from him again. I hope the comfort I gave him lessened his pain and that he spent his final days warmed by the inspiration of the Book.

A memorable call came one night in a totally different spirit.

"I'm going to kill you," a shrill voice declared.

"Brother, I'm saved," I said. "Ready to meet my God whenever my time comes."

"I've heard you preach. I won't tell you where. But I know you're a hypocrite and a liar. You're in this religious racket for the money. I hate fat, well-fed preachers."

"You're right, I am well-fed. Well-fed on the bread and water of the Lord."

"You'll never know when the bullet is coming. Maybe on the street. Maybe next time you preach. It could be anywhere, anytime."

"You take your gun and shoot me whenever you want. I have a place reserved for me in heaven. And you know where you're headed."

"Before I go to hell, I'll dance on your grave."

"God bless you," I said, "because God is the only one who can help you."

"Remember, preacher, it could be anytime, anywhere."

He broke the connection. I'm still alive and breathing and right with the Lord. I don't have a moment's worry about that wretched creature and his paranoid threat because I know that God is protecting me every second of my life.

"I'll give you a certified check for one million dollars if you'll declare publicly that you and Christ are phonies," was the astonishing opening remark I heard one night from another caller.

"I'll guarantee you a place in heaven and you can keep your million dollars," I said.

To add to my astonishment, the man gave me his name and address. I subsequently checked and it turned out the man was bona fide. He could well afford to write a check for a million dollars.

"I've made my fortune," he continued, "by believing that people are all greedy and self-seeking. I don't believe anybody can follow the teachings of Christ and become a rich man."

"Then you're ignorant. I could name you a thousand men in America who are millionaires and good Christians."

"They just pretend they're Christians."

"I've buried millionaires with the sure knowledge that they were going to heaven. Where are you going?"

"Think of it, preacher. One million dollars. You get it if I read in the paper tomorrow that you've called Christ the greatest phony that ever lived."

"All the money in the world wouldn't substitute for the joy and happiness that I've found since I came to Christ. You take your money and burn it for all the good it's going to do you with the Lord."

"You're a damn fool!" he said and broke the connection.

"This is Jesus Christ calling!" a well-modulated, educated voice said when I picked up the phone on another occasion.

"Where are you calling from? I didn't know they had telephones in heaven."

"I'm calling from a bar on Bourbon Street. I'm here observing the sinners."

"The Bible says for us to expect the return of Jesus to earth. But I don't think you're Jesus."

"Yes I am. You'll have to take my word for it."

"Can you walk on water?"

"No."

"If I buried you, would you rise again?"

"No."

"Can you show me the nail scars on your hands?"

"I've got a tattoo I can show you."

"I don't remember reading in the Bible about Jesus being tattooed."

"You'd be surprised how many people believe I really am Jesus."

"Not this ignorant Baptist preacher," I said, cutting the farcical conversation short.

Insomniacs are among my most frequent callers. Tossing and turning in bed, unable to lie down in peace, they phone me for solace. Countless times I've recited to them the short, simple verse from the Book of Proverbs:

"When thou liest down, thou shalt not be afraid: yea, thou shalt lie down, and thy sleep shall be sweet."

The verse is the most potent tranquilizer I know and those who have committed it to memory, repeating it several times when their heads hit the pillow, have no trouble sleeping.

My telephone ministry is a two-way affair. Among those I call every night is a widow in her eighties. She's in failing health, blind in one eye and suffering painfully from rheumatism. The conversation is a ritual between us, always brief and always pretty much the same.

"How was your day?"

"Fine, preacher."

"I just want you to know the Lord is looking after you."

"I know. It's so good to hear your voice. I can't really afford this telephone. I only keep it so I can talk to you. You're the only one who ever calls."

"Anything I can do for you?"

"Just call again tomorrow night and we'll have another nice little chat."

One evening I picked up the phone and heard a distant voice talking to me from Hong Kong. The call was from a soldier on leave after eleven months of fighting in Vietnam.

"Would you keep an eye on my girl?"

He told me her name and where she worked as a stripper on the street. I knew the girl well.

"I love her, preacher. It kills me every time I think of her taking her clothes off in front of all those men."

"It shames me, too, and it shames her in the sight of God. But I know she's being faithful. Every time I see her she reads your letters to me. All she talks about is how the two of you are going to get married when you come home."

"Will you marry us?"

"Certainly."

I performed the ceremony a few months later. The girl left the street and moved with her husband to a trailer park on the outskirts of New Orleans while he studied law at Tulane University.

About once a month I receive a call from a world-renowned movie star, who has asked me not to reveal her name. I met and witnessed to her during a Crusade I conducted at the Hollywood Palladium a few years ago.

"I just want to tell you I'm still right with the Lord," is her usual opening remark.

"Bless you."

I remember one of our conversations vividly. "They sent me a script today. It's going to be a filthy movie. I would have to do three nude scenes."

"You know how I feel about that."

"I turned it down. It cost me two hundred and fifty thousand dollars, but I couldn't go through with it."

"You made the right decision."

"I know. I feel so good inside, so strong and at peace with myself."

There aren't many stars in Hollywood whose religious convictions are hardy enough to throw away a fortune. But this is one star who realizes that faith is more valuable than a brimming bank account. And I'm happy to report that her career continues to flourish despite the fact that she will appear only in wholesome, family-oriented pictures.

Surprise constantly lurks at the other end of the wire. "I'm a Catholic priest," the voice said. "But I plan to leave the church. I want to get married."

I reminded him of the sacredness of his vows.

"I have a terrible struggle going on within me," he said. "But I've made up my mind."

I made an appointment to see him. He never explained why a Catholic priest would call on a Baptist preacher to discuss his soul-searing problem.

In a long series of discussions between us, he finally came to the conclusion that his work for God took precedence over his own personal satisfaction. He returned to the Church and is now a parish priest in a suburban Michigan community. We still talk frequently over the phone.

Some callers are eager to debate fine points of theology. But usually they are lost souls attempting to justify their reprehensible behavior.

One summer evening a woman called and told me: "I was raised in a strict Calvinist home. I believe that God created evil to offset and balance the good. Therefore, sin is a part of God's will. If God was truly a just God, then He would not send people to hell for being and doing what they were meant to do. If a Christian is lustful and evil, it is because God created him for this purpose. Man is predestined by fate. And man is not responsible for what he is."

I said, "The whole tradition of the Bible contradicts such a thesis. Every individual *is* responsible to God for his own actions and must answer to God accordingly. Man is only condemned because he rejects the healing power of faith and does not use his divinely imposed free will to come forth, be saved and grow each day in Christian living. The ultimate sin is to refuse to repent and trust God as your Lord and Savior."

The woman was unconvinced. She admitted that she was a prostitute and she was determined to continue leading her sinful life, accusing God rather than repenting.

Of all the calls I've received, the most inspiring came one evening about 7:30 P.M.

The voice on the line was young and enthusiastic. The boy identified himself as an electronics major at a midwestern university. He had thirty young men and women in his room at the dorm and he asked me if I would preach a sermon and lead them all to the Lord. He had an amplifier hooked up to the telephone.

The request was unusual, but the prospect of winning thirty souls to Christ, even on the telephone, was not an opportunity I could forsake.

Briefly, I told the story of my own conversion. And then I led them in prayer. I concluded with verses 7–9 from Chapter 14 of Romans:

"For none of us liveth to himself, and no man dieth to himself.

"For whether we live, we live unto the Lord; and whether we die, we die unto the Lord: whether we live therefore, or die, we are the Lord's.

"For to this end Christ both died, and rose, and revived, that he might be Lord both of the dead and living."

Several days later, a letter arrived at my office. It extended heartfelt thanks and it was signed by all thirty of the college students who had used the telephone to revitalize their Christian lives.

Life, death, salvation or damnation—only the Lord knows what new adventure will come tonight when the phone rings in the office of the Chaplain of Bourbon Street.

14

THE ROARING LION AMONG US

The Bible calls him by many names. Satan, devil, Abaddon, Apollyon, Beelzebub, Belial, Adversary, Dragon, Serpent and the Prince and Power of the Air.

His crimes riddle Scripture. He tempted Eve and Christ, he perverted the word, opposed God's work, hindered God's servants and the spreading of the gospel, ensnared the wicked, deceived the nations, brought sin into the world and was responsible for the fall of man.

The First Epistle of Peter 5:8 warns: "Be sober, be vigilant; because your adversary the devil, as a roaring lion, walketh about, seeking whom he may devour."

In America today, intellectuals and psuedo-intellectuals hide behind a veneer of sophistication and ridicule the idea of the existence of a personal devil. But, in a recent survey, 72 per cent of Americans said they believed in Satan.

An editorial in the *Capital Baptist*, weekly publication of the District of Columbia Baptist Convention, has suggested a "Devil is Alive Movement" as a counterpart of the highly publicized "God is Dead Movement."

"Keep your eyes open—your life clean—the DEVIL IS ALIVE," editor James O. Duncan wrote. "There is no question about this. Those people who don't believe this have already been bamboozled by the biggest bamboozler of them all.

"The devil is so shifty—so crafty—so sly—so treacherous. He can make you think you are Christian in your actions when all the time you could be hurting the cause you intended to help.

"The devil works. He works hardest on those that are the most religious. The non-believer he already has.

"The devil has already convinced too many people that they should act without regard to others in society; that they ought to live for themselves and forget others; that sin is just having a good time and anyone that isn't for a good time is just a fuddy-dud.

"The devil never gets around to saying that there will be a day of reckoning; that every man must give an account of his sins; that freedom does not exist apart from God.

"Keep your eyes open—the devil is alive."

No one in this day and age pictures the devil as he usually was represented in the Middle Ages—a snorting, fire-breathing creature with horns, a forked tail and cloven hoofs. The devil is too wily for that. As the supreme spirit of evil, Satan has no need of disguises. He lives in the hearts of men everywhere.

If you doubt it, look at the front page of this morning's newspaper with its stories of war, assassination, crime—a daily log of demon-inspired events that chips away at our national morality. Read about Satan in your favorite magazine, ogle the pictures of the brazen girls who pose in the nude and memorize those articles which urge premarital and extra-marital sexual relationships. Visit your bookstore and pick up the latest best seller with its clinical descriptions of unnatural sex cribbed from the Marquis de Sade. Go to the movies or watch television for an outpouring of unremitting violence, brutality, greed and irreverence to God.

Better yet, visit Bourbon Street and see how the devil has captured the souls of thousands of men and women. Any night on Bourbon Street will do, but if you really want to see the devil in action come to New Orleans during Mardi Gras.

The world-famous Mardi Gras pumps millions of dollars into the city every year and hotels are booked months in advance by tourists from all over the globe eager to participate in the festivities.

On television the public only sees the floats and parades along Canal Street, but Mardi Gras in reality is one vast orgy of sex and booze. During the celebration, Bourbon Street booms as at no other time. Portable stands selling whiskey and beer are set up on the sidewalks outside the honky-tonks. Among the masked revelers who flood the street are hardened homosexuals who lure small boys into acts of perversion, men who reach out to fondle the breasts of strange women. The prostitutes have more business than they can handle.

Mardi Gras is one mighty explosion of sin, stage-managed by the devil.

I believe that the people of Sodom and Gomorrah, if they could be resurrected and visit New Orleans during Mardi Gras, would by unanimous vote request that they be sent back to hell. I think that Mardi Gras is a time when even the devil is ashamed of his own followers.

During the first year of my ministry on Bourbon Street, I was foolish enough to think I could do a job for the Lord during Mardi Gras. I brought ten Christian men and women with me to my headquarters (we even carried our own lunches, because people are so thick on the street you could faint from hunger and it would take you three blocks to fall). We set up a loudspeaker, sang gospel hymns, gave our testimony and passed out tracts. The crowds laughed and ignored us. Infuriated, I went to a nearby funeral home, got a casket and placed it in front of the office with the lid open and a mirror propped inside. I was hoping that some of the passers-by would be shocked into the realization that they were going to die as sinners enthralled by the devil, that they were going to die without salvation.

It didn't work. The next day I found the casket filled with beer cans and empty whiskey bottles.

"I know there is a devil for two reasons," said Billy Sunday. "First, the Bible declares it; and second, I have done business with him."

So have I—every day of my ministry on Bourbon Street.

I don't kid myself, people can be happy with Satan, but they really have to concentrate.

Here's a blueprint for those ready to make a pact with the devil:

Forget about the ten commandments! With Satan as your god the commandments do not apply. You can kill, steal, commit adultery, lie, curse, envy your neighbor and ignore your parents.

Forget about Calvary! Ignore that God loves you and gave His Son to die for you. Ignore that God sent not his Son into the world to condemn you but that you, through Him, might be saved.

Forget about health! Live fast. Ride the needle. Smoke three packs of cigarettes a day. Get drunk. Don't sleep. Stay on the move. Satan promotes fast living.

Forget about friends and family! Bring your wife, sister and daughter to Bourbon Street. Make strippers out of them. After the shows, sell them as prostitutes. After all, if someone else hadn't brought his wife, daughter or sister you couldn't lust over the current belles.

But also remember these "don'ts" when you make your pact with the devil:

Don't die! Because if you do you'll end up in hell.

Don't lose your health! Venereal diseases, lung cancer, alcoholism, narcotics addiction are hard to cure.

Don't run out of money! Satan can make you happy only so long as you have plenty of cash to spend. Don't expect to hold a good-paying job, because Satan's power will disqualify you.

Don't cry out for help! Satan has no time to help his foolish victims.

Only by coming to Christ can you turn a deaf ear to the siren song of Satan. And you come to Christ by being saved.

Being saved is far more than a one-time profession of faith at a revival meeting.

A deacon at a week-long Crusade I conducted in Tennessee asked me, "What do we do with all the souls you've led to Christ after you leave town? What if they become backsliders?"

"Then you bring them to Christ again, again and again," I told him. "It's like taking a bath. One bath doesn't mean you never have to take another one."

When someone is truly saved he has achieved salvation, which means deliverance, which means born again, which means transformed, which means coming from darkness to light, coming from a sinful condition to a saved condition.

Anyone can be saved. But first, you must realize that you are sinful, that you are lost without Christ. Christ came to seek and save those who are lost.

The word "saved" is shorthand for salvation.

Salvation is spiritual deliverance from the burden of sin, deliverance from guilt, anxiety and fear. For those who are truly saved, it means a 180-degree turnaround in their lives, it means deliverance from hell and a sure place in heaven. It means deliverance from the problem and preoccupation with self. God put men on earth to live for each other in a spirit of brotherhood.

Being saved means new strength, fresh commitment and a way of life that makes you feel you are born again.

Putting your life in Christ's hands is the most important and meaningful decision you can make. Your immortal soul is the prize. But you can be sure that the enemy of your soul, the devil, will seek by every means to confuse your mind and undermine your faith.

But with Christ you defeat the devil. There is no greater joy in all the world than to know Christ personally, to know your sins are forgiven and to have peace in your soul. You are born again—born of the Spirit. A miracle has taken place in your life. You are a new creature. "Therefore if any man be in Christ, he is a new creature: old things are passed away; behold, all things are become new" (II Corinthians 5:17). God, the Creator of the universe, has become your Father. Now, for the first time, you are considered a child of God and heaven is your eternal home.

Although your decision to become a Christian is great and important, it is not all. It is but the beginning of a new life in Christ. When you are saved you are not immediately a full-grown Christian, but a "babe in Christ." As a "baby," you are commanded to "grow" (II Peter 3:18). Everybody loves babies, but nobody wants them to stay in the nursery forever. Only by growing spiritually can you please God and glorify Him in your life.

In order to grow to maturity as a Christian, you must be loyal and obedient to the commands of Christ. He said, "If ye love me, keep my commandments" (John 14:15). So that you may know what the Lord expects of His disciples, here are some of the essential requirements:

1. Be baptized. Baptism is the first step of obedience for a new Christian. The first public act in the ministry of Jesus was His baptism by John the Baptist in the river Jordan. The New Testament teaches that baptism is an outward sign of an inward change. It is a public confession and testimony of what has already taken place in your heart. Baptism is a burial and a resurrection. We are buried with Christ (immersed in water) in the likeness of His death, and we are raised with Christ in the likeness of His resurrection. Not only does baptism picture the death, burial and resurrection of Christ, it also pictures the burial of the old sinful life and the resurrection of a new life in Christ. As a believer, you should be baptized not in order to be saved but because you are saved. It is a witness to your faith in Christ.

2. Read your Bible daily. Jesus said, "Man shall not live by bread alone, but by every word that proceedeth out of the mouth of God" (Matthew 4:4). Just as you need food to sustain physical life, so you need spiritual food (the Bible) to maintain spiritual life. Begin with the New Testament and read the Gospel of John or Mark. Follow this with the Book of Acts. Next, read Paul's Epistle to the Romans. The entire New Testament can be read in three months by reading three chapters a day. By reading three chapters of the Old Testament and one chapter of the New Testament each day, the whole Bible can be read in a year. Set aside a few moments early in each day for Bible study. Look for promises to claim and commands to obey, examples to follow and sins to avoid. Memorize key verses such as II Timothy 4:18, "And the Lord shall deliver me from every evil work, and will preserve me unto his heavenly kingdom: to whom be glory for ever and ever." Your growth as a Christian will be directly related to your personal application of the word of God.

3. Pray every day. "Men ought always to pray," Jesus said in Luke 18:1. In another place we read, "Pray without ceasing" (I Thessalonians 5:17). You should form the habit of praying daily for definite people and specific things. A prayer list may prove helpful in making your prayers more meaningful. There is nothing too great and nothing too small to take to the Lord in prayer. Thank God for all He has done for you. Ask Him for the strength and help you need to live for Jesus Christ.

4. Witness for Christ. Let's look at the soul-winning approach of Jesus:

a) He believed that all men are worth saving.

b) He won their confidence.

c) He stimulated their curiosity into a thirst for spiritual knowledge.

d) He confronted them boldly and inescapably with the question of sin.

e) He led them to turn from sin to faith in Himself.

f) He encouraged them to share their experience of salvation with someone else.

Successful soul-winning demands that we sacrifice and agonize over lost souls. Genuine love and concern must undergird each presentation of the gospel. Knowing the mechanics of soul-winning is not enough. Soul-winners must be concerned with lost individuals, not merely as statistics or potential church members, but as persons who are trying to find themselves, trying to find out who they are and where they are going.

Evangelist Dwight L. Moody took soul-winning so seriously

that he would not sleep at night until he had shared the saving power of Jesus Christ with at least one other person. Amy Carmichel, another dedicated soul-winner, prayed:

> *Oh for a passion of souls*
> *Oh for a pity that yearns*
> *Oh for a love that loves unto death*
> *Oh for a heart that burns.*

The greatest work in the world is soul-winning, and every Christian can and should bring others to the Savior. Jesus said, ". . . ye shall be witnesses unto me" (Acts 1:8). Try to speak naturally and cheerfully every day to someone about Christ. Proverbs 11:30 says, ". . . he that winneth souls is wise." Remember that you witness by what you do as well as by what you say. At home, at work, at school, there should be something about you that's different—love, patience, understanding. Then tell someone about Him who makes the difference.

Always ask yourself: am I in the right relationship to Christ? Rededicate yourself to Him if Satan has led you astray.

Claim God's Spirit. Ask Him to fill you, lead you, and use you to win souls to Jesus.

5. Tithe your income. Giving a tenth of your income is the Biblical method of supporting God's work. The Bible tells us, "Upon the first day [Sunday] of the week let every one of you lay by him in store, as God hath prospered him" (I Corinthians 16:2). God says to bring the tithe into the "storehouse," meaning the local church. Your church is your storehouse of spiritual food, blessing and service, so this is the proper place to give your tithe. "Bring ye all the tithes into the storehouse . . . and prove me now herewith, saith the Lord of hosts, if I will not open you the windows of heaven, and pour you out a blessing, that there shall not be room enough to

receive it" (Malachi 3:10). The right use of money is a test of character. If you are dishonest toward God in money matters you cannot grow spiritually.

6. Attend church regularly. The Christian life should be a family affair in which we enjoy fellowship with our Heavenly Father and with each other. Every Christian should unite with a local Bible-believing church and share its worship, its fellowship and its witness. If Jesus loved the church enough to die for it, this is sufficient reason for us to love and support it. Regular church attendance should be as much a habit as eating. "Not forsaking the assembling of ourselves together" (Hebrews 10:25) is a clear command of the word of God. In church you will hear God's word read, explained and applied to your everyday problems of life. God has ordained men to minister and preach His word. Every Christian, young and old, needs the inspiration and information gained in a church worship service. If you try to live the Christian life alone, failure will result. In unity there is strength. Through the church, you can render service to a lost and dying world.

Time is running out for all of us.

The clock ticks away the moments of our lives.

The devil is a tireless foe and believes that time is on his side.

Remember Billy Sunday's words, "I have done business with [the devil]."

We all have, not only on Bourbon Street in New Orleans, but on the facsimiles of Bourbon Street which exist all over the world.

Only by a Christian commitment can you defeat Satan and claim the Lord in everlasting life.

When should you make that commitment?

The answer is now!

15

A HEARTBEAT FROM ETERNITY

During a Crusade I was conducting in Hollywood a few years ago, I took time off one afternoon to visit the lavish pink stucco home of Jayne Mansfield. I thought Miss Mansfield, as the supreme sex symbol of her time, might be ready to come to the Lord. Her career in movies had been fading and she was reduced to personal appearances around the country in low-grade nightclubs. Her performance was an affront to God. She writhed and wiggled on the stage, made suggestive remarks, told off-color stories. Her only stock in trade was an ample bosom and a Junoesque figure.

A maid answered the door and I introduced myself. "Please tell Miss Mansfield I'm here to talk to her about the Lord."

I wasn't invited into the house. So I waited patiently outside. In a few moments the maid returned and told me, "Miss Mansfield is sorry, but she has no time to talk to you."

"Did you tell her I wanted to see her about the most important thing in her life? Did you tell her I wanted to talk to her about God?"

"Yes, sir," the maid answered, "but she just doesn't have the time."

No time to talk about the Lord. How tragic, I thought.

A few months later, barreling over a Mississippi highway, Jayne Mansfield was decapitated in a gory automobile accident. She died, I'm sorry to say, as a sinner. She died lost and damned. Had she had the time for me that day her entire life might have been changed. She might have found her eternal resting place in heaven.

Contrast her death with the last conscious act of Senator Robert F. Kennedy, brutally struck down by an assassin's bullet in a Los Angeles hotel in 1968. As Senator Kennedy lay on the kitchen floor of the hotel, a busboy pressed a crucifix to his chest. The senator's eyes seemed to flicker in appreciation. He was dead several hours later, but in his last moment of awareness he recognized the supreme power of the Lord. The senator died saved and rests in heaven today.

"To every thing there is a season, and a time to every purpose under the heaven: A time to be born, and a time to die . . ." the Bible says in Ecclesiastes 3:1-2.

The people I meet on Bourbon Street are like people everywhere. They hate to think about death and they have no time for religion except when they're dying. Then they call for me: "Get the preacher. Get the preacher." When they're dying, everybody has time. If the Lord is good enough for them when they're dying, He ought to be good enough for them while they're still living.

I sometimes wonder why people cling so tenaciously to life when their lives are hell on earth and they spend their days committing slow suicide.

"We continue to kill ourselves in spite of great medical achievements that promise to prolong life," writes Dr. Peter J. Steincrohn in his excellent book *How to Stop Killing Yourself.* "Thousands die of cancer who might have been cured. Of heart disease. Of chronic alcoholism. Of high blood pressure. Of overwork—or of underwork.

"Infinite and varied are the ways you and I find to commit

slow suicide. For it is still true that too many of us needlessly shorten the days of our years.

"Man is his own worst enemy. Events since the expulsion from the Garden of Eden have proved it; my own experience in the study of medicine has confirmed it."

There are two forces that contend for supremacy inside every man—the desire for self-destruction and the desire for self-preservation. With Christ activating his soul, no man need fear which force will emerge triumphant. Christ not only promises everlasting life, but a sweet life of abundance and happiness on this earth.

Yet there are millions who ignore the message.

One doctor has referred to our decade as the "Suicidal Sixties." And he's right. Suicide has risen 50 per cent in the last ten years. This year, 200,000 Americans will attempt to take their lives. More than 25,000 will succeed.

Most alarming of all is that suicide has become the number-one killer among our college students. The rate among youngsters has soared to approximately one hundred attempts per day. Two teen-agers a day manage to blot out their lives.

"Let's not hide a growing problem," says Dr. Willard D. Boaz, assistant professor at Western Reserve University. "Why should youngsters in a nation such as ours suddenly begin to take their lives at a rate three times what it was in 1960?"

The reason is no secret. Those youngsters do not have Christ in their lives.

The most horrible aspect of drug addiction, poisoning and automobile accidents is that no one knows how many people are using these methods with suicide in mind. Health officials estimate that about 10 per cent of all fatal car accidents and 15 per cent of all home accidents (poisonings primarily) are not accidents at all, but "hidden" suicide attempts.

Many large American cities have established anti-suicide

centers. They receive thousands of calls each year from people on the verge of killing themselves.

Christ could save them all if they would but come to Him.

To overcome their suicidal tendencies, thousands in this country each year visit psychiatrists. Such people have dead souls; something fundamental has gone out of their lives. But, instead of spending twenty-five to fifty dollars an hour with a psychiatrist, they can let the Lord into their hearts. Jesus is the world's best psychiatrist. He always has a cure.

I've found that the chance of sudden death often brings a sinner to the Lord posthaste.

I was on a plane recently, traveling from Little Rock, Arkansas, to New Orleans. I was sitting in my seat reading my Bible when the man next to me offered me a cigar. I said, "No, thanks, the Lord has saved me from that."

When the stewardess came by taking orders for drinks, the man said, "Have a cocktail."

"No, the Lord also saved me from that."

Spotting my Bible, he said, "I don't believe in God."

As I was about to answer, the plane hit an air pocket, and the big aircraft started bucking furiously. I began humming "Nearer My God to Thee."

My seatmate's knuckles were white, he was holding on for dear life. I sang a verse of "Lord, I'm Coming Home."

"Aren't you scared?" the man asked.

"When you're saved, as I am, you have no fear of death."

He tried to summon up his courage. "Just because I'm scared," he said, "you're not going to convert me."

"Take a look out of that window. What do you see?" I asked.

"A wing and two motors."

"If those motors go, mister, I'll have you for the Lord before we hit the ground."

I wasn't mistaken. White knuckles and all, he kept darting his eyes from the motors to my Bible. At last he said, "You're right, I'm ready to be saved."

Through miles of turbulence, we prayed together and I won that man to the Lord.

When it comes to death, you don't meet any heroes. There are no tough guys when death is imminent. Some men who've shouted the loudest against God while they were healthy cry the loudest when they're dying. "Oh, God, have mercy on me. Forgive me, God." I've heard that pitiful plea many times. You never meet an athiest in a terminal cancer ward or in a foxhole.

When I preached at An Khe, Vietnam, I won to Christ more than one hundred soldiers of the First Cavalry Division. After the services were over, the men were sent on a search-and-destroy mission. Seventeen of them were killed. On my return from Vietnam someone asked me if my preaching to the troops served any useful purpose. I replied, "The best way to measure if I did any good or not is when I get to heaven. Then I'll ask those seventeen boys."

Everywhere I preach, I talk about the pressing, inevitable reality of death. And I don't pull any punches.

Funeral services will be held, I tell audiences, for Mr. Neglect. He starved himself to death by staying away from the Lord, by not reading God's word, by not praying and by not witnessing. He slipped away gradually, almost unnoticed. His pallbearers were: Didn't Care, Too Tired, Company Coming, Nothing to Do, No Time, Sleep Awhile Longer, Unconcern.

In Ennis, Texas, I preached at a revival and helped to strengthen spiritually the owner of a restaurant called Dan's Townhouse. The man dedicated his life to the Lord on a Monday night. During the next week he held a coffee hour for me every evening so that the businessmen of the town could come by and talk about the things of the Lord. A week after he was spiritually revived, the man died of a heart attack. He was dead at the age of forty-two. But he spent the last week of his life serving the Lord. He's still remembered in Ennis as a godly Christian who spent his final days on earth working for Christ. His reward in heaven is certain. It's never too late for a sinner to repent.

To dramatize my message about death while I was broadcasting one night on radio station WWL in New Orleans, I obtained a recording of a human heartbeat and played it at the end of my sermon. I let the sound of the beating heart repeat itself for a long moment. And then I asked my audience: "How far are you from death?" Then I had the sound turned up again on the beating heart. Thousands of letters poured in as a result of that broadcast, all of them alive with the sudden realization that life was fragile. All these people asked for Christ to come into their lives.

The quickest way to kill any conversation, I've discovered, is to bring up the subject of death. People just don't like to talk or think about it. Have you ever heard a hostess call her friends and say, "Come on over to the house so we can talk about dying." Has a group of teen-agers ever gathered together with the invitation, "Let's have a party in the playroom; we'll have some moon pie and cokes and we'll talk about who's going to die next"? Ever hear of anybody doing that? Did you ever get a card in the mail saying, "Merry Death, Happy Dying"?

In our world today, everything is geared to living, everything is geared to excitement. The thought of death lies buried deep in the subconscious.

One day I spotted a disheveled looking man walking down Bourbon Street carrying a brown package under his arm. I could see it wasn't milk because the neck of the bottle was too long. I was standing there with my Bible. I stopped him and asked: "Where are you going?"

"To my car," he said.

"I mean, when you die."

"I'm not dead yet. Can't you see I'm alive?"

"I know, but you're going to die. The Book says you're going to die. Before you go don't you want to be saved?"

"No."

"Don't you believe in the Lord and Savior?"

"Sure."

"Then why not come to Him now?"

"All right, preacher, if you really think I'm worth saving."

"Let's kneel down here and pray."

"Right here on the street?"

"Yes."

"This is the wrong place."

"You mean it's the right place for the bottle, but the wrong place for the Bible?"

"I don't exactly mean that."

"You don't think you can be saved on Bourbon Street?"

"No."

"Where do you think you're going to be saved?"

He pointed to the steeple of St. Louis Cathedral.

I asked, "Do you believe you have to go to church to be saved?"

"Yes."

"Do you have to go to a funeral home to die?"

"There you go, talking about dying again."

And he took off down the street. The subject of death was too distressing for him to contemplate.

On one of my trips to Texas I talked to a man on Governor John B. Connally's staff. "Tell me about Governor Connally,"

I said. "He was riding in the car with President Kennedy when he was assassinated in Dallas. What was the governor thinking about when the President was dead in the back seat and he was there with a bullet in his own body? What was the governor really thinking about?"

He said, "The governor was thinking about the President, about the nation, about the state of Texas, about his family."

"Come on," I persisted, "what was the governor really thinking about?"

"Well," he answered candidly, "every time the governor gets to that part of the story, he breaks down and starts crying."

Of course. Whether you're the governor of Texas or a shoe-shine boy in the French Quarter, when you've got a bullet in your body and the angel of death is hovering over you, you're not pledging allegiance to the flag, you're not reciting the preamble to the Constitution, you're concerned about where you're going to spend eternity.

The saddest moment of my life came several years ago when I stood outside the glass-walled nursery of a New Orleans hospital and watched a team of doctors and nurses work eight hours on the tiny body of my newborn son. Finally, the doctor removed his stethoscope and pointed up to heaven. I knew then our little boy hadn't made it. I knew I'd never get a chance to play football with him, raise him in a Christian home, and perhaps guide him into a life dedicated to preaching the gospel.

Robert Grey Harrington entered the kingdom of God before he had the precious chance to embark on the adventure of life. Joyce and I have never questioned the Lord's judgment in taking him from us so soon.

Riding down in the hospital elevator after our little Bobby's life had so quickly been snuffed out I met a nine-year-old boy in the lobby.

"Are you Brother Bob Harrington?" the boy asked.

"Yes, son, I am."

"I'm an altar boy in church and I hear them talking about heaven and hell and eternity. Could you help me? I'd like to know how far off is eternity."

"It's strange you should ask that question because upstairs a few moments ago my son died and began his first ten thousand years with the Lord. The best way for me to answer your question about eternity is for you to put your hand over your heart."

The boy did so.

"What do you hear?" I asked.

"My heart beating."

"That's right, son. That's it. How far off is heaven? How far off is hell? How far off is eternity? Just one heartbeat. Just one heartbeat."

The boy looked at me with new comprehension.

"I'm just one heartbeat from eternity," he said.

I turned away and walked quickly out of the hospital. Still thinking of my son, I didn't want anyone to see the tears streaming down my face. For him, there were no heartbeats left. Eternity had already claimed his soul.

16

REACHING OUT FROM
BOURBON STREET

The road from Bourbon Street has led me to every corner of the globe.

I've preached at revivals and conducted Crusades from Paris, France, to Vietnam and in almost every one of the fifty states. There's nothing I enjoy more than witnessing for the Lord. If possible, I'd preach the word of Jesus from Red Square in Moscow.

As I have found, trained and organized a growing team of dedicated young Christians to aid me in my Bourbon Street ministry, I've been able to devote more time to the task I believe the Lord has set for me—evangelizing the world!

Evil and sin are not confined to Bourbon Street. There is a need everywhere for a voice preaching the tested virtues of two thousand years of Christianity.

Therefore, I'm ready to hop a jet to Honolulu and address an audience of twenty thousand or ride mule-back into the hills of Georgia to preach before a gathering of the Ku Klux Klan.

The hooded knights of the Klan got more than they bargained for when I was invited to address one of their meetings a few summers ago.

I told them I knew a place where there was no integration problem. "When you fellows get to hell," I declared, "you won't care whether you're burning between an Eskimo and a Negro. Instead of worrying about civil rights you should be concerned about spiritual rights."

One of the white-robed klansmen called out, "We were misled about you. We thought you were a preacher who'd see things our way."

"I don't know where you got your information about me, but I haven't misled you," I fumed. "There really won't be an integration problem in hell."

"How do you know?" the man asked.

"Die without coming to Christ and you'll find out."

An angry murmur bubbled up from the crowd. But it didn't worry me.

I said, "You fellows can lash me to one of your burning crosses and I'll go up in flames preaching, as Christ did, compassion for the poor, tolerance and understanding between all men."

I turned on my heel and walked away, leaving those misguided souls in their bedsheets to ponder what I had told them.

The toughest town I ever preached in was Macon, Mississippi. The crowds were small during the first two nights of my revival—and I knew why. Negroes weren't permitted to attend.

I got on the radio and announced that my revival would be open to anyone, regardless of color. The broadcast created a storm of protest. I was accused of being a Communist. ("He wears a red tie, doesn't he?") I was charged with being an integrationist sent from the North by sinister forces to stir things up.

There was a fence surrounding the fairgrounds where I was

preaching and the night of my radio broadcast the sheriff, his police force, many townspeople and some preachers stood at the entrance and turned away the Negroes who had come to hear me.

I was ashamed of the hatred and ill-will I saw in Macon, particularly ashamed that ministers of God had conspired to prevent black men and women from hearing the message of the Lord.

I was in Philadelphia, Mississippi, shortly after the murder of civil rights workers James Chaney, Andrew Goodman and Michael Schwerner. At the time I arrived, the town was flooded with FBI men, who were searching for the bodies of the three victims. I went to the spot where the young men were last seen. I knelt down and prayed that God would reveal where they had been buried. I've never felt the power of the Lord inside me as strong as I did on that occasion. Less than twenty-four hours after I had prayed, the authorities found the three bodies.

In the name of Jesus, I am willing to take on any sinner and fight for every righteous cause.

When I arrived in Memphis, Tennessee, for a revival, I obtained through a friend the unlisted telephone number of Elvis Presley.

I phoned Elvis at his Graceland mansion and invited him to appear at my interdenominational service and give his life to the Lord so that everyone would know he was saved. I knew that if he made a public decision for Jesus, an unimaginable number of people throughout the world would also be influenced for Christ.

On the phone, Elvis avoided giving me a direct answer to my invitation. He said he wasn't sure he could make it.

Word, meantime, had spread through Memphis that Elvis

might appear and the first night of the revival Ellis Auditorium was filled to capacity.

The people of Elvis' Assembly of God church love him dearly, though they haven't approved of his decision to stop attending church. Elvis claims that his attendance would cause a stampede for autographs and disrupt the services. Yet his fellow parishioners believe he has the potential to make the greatest evangelist the world has ever known if he would publicly dedicate his life to Christ and go to work for the Lord.

Elvis had not yet appeared when I walked to the center of the stage and began speaking. I made no secret of my feelings.

"There's one outstanding Memphian that I hoped would be here tonight," I told the crowd. "I called him this afternoon to extend a personal invitation and although he hasn't arrived we still have hope that Elvis Presley will realize that he should be here in the auditorium worshiping with us tonight.

"I know that he's done a lot for the community chest and other worthwhile charities, and has given a good deal of money to the church. But he hasn't given anything of himself. This may come as a shock to many people, but it is a hard fact that Elvis Presley is paying off the church to leave him alone! He doles out just enough money to the budget and building funds so that the preachers will be afraid to bother him about getting right with the Lord.

"Elvis Presley could win more young people to Christ in the instant it would take him to walk down the aisle and profess his intentions to dedicate the rest of his life to God than many evangelists could win in a lifetime.

"Elvis is unquestionably the symbol of this generation and if he possessed the courage to give up an extravagant life of fame and fortune—and it would take hard-core courage for any normal human being to transform his living habits from those of a king to those of a servant—it would make it much easier for other people to give up their own comfortable sins.

"A definite mark has been made on the world by the words 'Elvis Presley,' but he could make a much more impressive mark with a Bible in his hands than by holding a guitar and singing 'You Ain't Nothing But a Hound Dog.'

"There comes a time when a person has to make the final decision about just how he's going to use the talents that have been given to him. If Elvis Presley doesn't make the right decision tonight, he may never feel the need again, and that would be a tragedy. This is the most crucial night in this young man's life because he has already chosen by his presence or absence from this meeting what he considers most important: his belief in the Lord or his privacy."

I paused. Thousands of eyes turned toward the entrance of the auditorium. Elvis, it was obvious, wasn't going to appear.

I concluded by telling the crowd:

"It's clear that Elvis Presley won't be here tonight. We know that for ten years the force of God has been pulling at his heart and I pray that one day he will wake up to the fact that the Lord can do much more for him than Colonel Parker has ever done."

I'm still waiting for Elvis to make a public declaration of his faith. So is the Lord.

The FBI has a list of its Ten Most Wanted Men. I do, too. I fervently believe that if my Ten Most Wanted Men made decisions for Christ their influence would be overwhelming. These ten widely known men could become powerhouses for God and reclaim America.

The men on my list, in addition to Elvis Presley, are the President of the United States, Frank Sinatra, Dean Martin (he could start by changing his image as a perpetual drunk),

United Automobile Workers President Walter Reuther, Los Angeles Dodgers pitcher Don Drysdale, Hugh Hefner (how many copies would the publisher of *Playboy* sell if he removed the pictures of nude girls and articles urging sexual permissiveness?), Johnny Carson (he could better entertain his late-night audience without the tasteless blue material he so often uses), billionaire Howard Hughes (what a force for good his money could be if it were used for the things of the Lord instead of buying up Las Vegas gambling casinos) and Dr. Timothy Leary, the apostle of LSD and hero of the hippies.

There are hundreds of other names I could add to the list— but those ten will do for a start.

I do not intend the list to be taken in a derogatory way. I've named these particular men because through their influence they hold the pulse of the nation. I'm certain that all of them are religious individuals, each in his own way.

The purpose of the list is to call attention to what is most needed for a spiritual revival in America. We need strong leaders who are idolized and respected by the public to take a clear-cut, unequivocal stand for Christian living.

I feel that these key men could shake America out of its religious indifference if they would publicly announce themselves for Christ.

The religious beliefs of celebrities are of enormous consequence. World-wide headlines were snared when Beatle John Lennon called his singing group "more popular than Jesus." How many of the millions of teen-age fans who follow the Beatles were led astray, how many felt justified in cutting themselves off from Christ because of the remark?

Lennon was widely criticized for his statement, but what he said was true. I admire him for saying it. Lennon reminds me of the people on Bourbon Street. You don't find many hypocrites there. They tell the truth, bad as it might be. Of course the Beatles are more popular among young people than Jesus, but Ringo, George, Paul and John are not as powerful. Not by any stretch of the imagination. It's also interesting to reflect that the Beatles triggered an international fad for Indian guru Maharishi Mahesh Yogi. Despite their fame and riches, the Beatles had not achieved inner tranquillity. They went to India, sat at the feet of the guru and in time announced their disenchantment with transcendental meditation. How much easier, how much more rewarding it would be for the Beatles to accept Christ. If they did, their spiritual problems would disappear.

Mia Farrow and other Hollywood stars followed the Beatles' trek to India in the search for solace of the soul. But, as I told an audience in Los Angeles sprinkled with many well-known movie and television personalities, "Join me in Christ. Jesus is my producer and He's never had a flop. My writers are the best the world has ever seen. And what a script they wrote. From Genesis to Revelations, you've never read more thrilling and inspiring words."

In every city I visit I make it a point to tour the local bars and skin mills. I feel at home there. I often find it easier to work in nightclubs than to get the attention of high-steeple, few-people church crowds. Most of the people who frequent the nightclubs wouldn't be caught dead sitting under a steeple on Sunday morning.

In Jacksonville, Florida, a ring of scantily clad go-go girls surrounded me while I preached about Satan. "Sometimes the devil is black-haired, sometimes a blonde, sometimes only her hairdresser knows for sure."

A young man approached me and said he thought a preacher didn't belong in a nightclub.

"Why not?" I asked him. "There are plenty of Baptists, Methodists and other Christians in the place."

Then a heckler called out "sooey." Without batting an eye, I said, "A pig always lets you know which side he's on."

In Atlanta, Georgia, I preached in a dive known for its topless dancers. Five girls had just finished cavorting to the cheers of a semi-sober crowd.

"Hey," I said, "you're going to enjoy me, aren't you? Why not get excited for God?" I looked at a bald-headed, elderly man sitting with a teen-aged B-girl. "I may not be as much fun as she is, but I won't give you a guilt complex."

I didn't tell the crowd they were bad people, only that mine was a better way. "This is just an overnight kick here. Mine gets better and better."

The next day, the Atlanta *Journal* reported, "Reverend Harrington got more applause when he left the stage than the topless go-go girls did. After he spoke, the management asked him back on Saturday night 'when we'll have more people.' The result was worth seeing. So was the Chaplain of Bourbon Street."

When I was in Detroit, I toured the burlesque houses hoping to stir the souls of the city's strippers. A vice squad detective would have received a warmer welcome. Doors slammed shut on me at almost every step in the tenderloin area of lower Third Street. After being rebuffed at one strip joint, I told a reporter who was accompanying me, "If I'd stepped up to that window with a submachine gun and a breastplate, I wouldn't have stirred them up as much as I do with my Bible. When you walk over to somebody and pull this Book on them, it's like you just said 'stick 'em up.'"

I could understand why the burlesque house managers were reluctant to let me in. When somebody buys a ticket to see a skin show, he doesn't want to get preached to. But a Christian messenger has to keep trying to reach such people.

The next night, at the Masonic Auditorium, I told Detroiters that their city was relatively clean except for the topless bars and burlesque houses. Then I reminded them that in 1788 Edward Gibbon wrote in *The Decline and Fall of the Roman Empire* that there were five reasons for that fall: the rapid increase of divorce—the undermining of the dignity and sanctity of the home, which is the basis of human society. Higher and higher taxes and the spending of public money for free bread and circuses for the populace. The mad craze for pleasure; sports becoming every year more exciting and more brutal. The building of gigantic armaments when the real enemy was within—the decadence of the people. The decay of religion—faith fading into mere form and losing touch with life, becoming impotent to guide the people.

Then I asked: "Are there lessons here for us today?"

At a hippie hangout in San Francisco, I told it like it was to a mob of long-haired dropouts from society: "Adults are sinners who can't very well lead *you* away from sin. Most of you are rebels without a cause. You're hungering after leaders, and don't know who to follow. So you've been led astray by false prophets. I'll tell you who your leader should be—Jesus! He can put direction and meaning into your lives."

Someone shouted out, "Why are we condemned for wearing beards? Didn't Jesus wear a beard?"

"Certainly, but He was clean, too."

In Lawton, Oklahoma, Police Chief Alford Hennessee took me on a tour of the city's night life. The small town has seventy-eight taverns and twenty-seven private drinking clubs. It's been dubbed by some as "Sin City, USA."

One of the clubs I visited was jammed with GIs from a

neighboring Army base. I got up and preached a brief message:

"I think most of you soldiers would just as soon be in church if you realized how much fun practicing Christians are having. You're away from home and you're lonely and you're afraid. Many of you, I know, are headed for Vietnam.

"But sitting around and drinking beer and ogling girls is sinful. Anything you do that doesn't glorify God is sinful.

"Every one of the girls who works here tries to justify herself to me. One said she couldn't get a job anywhere else. Today they are go-go girls—but what will they be next month, next year? Will they be hung up on the bottle, flipping pills, breaking up a marriage?"

Four of the soldiers and two of the go-go girls met me outside afterwards. All came forth and gave themselves to Christ.

In Las Vegas I strolled through the plush casinos watching sinners throw their money away. New Orleans has the toughest sin, Las Vegas the fanciest. I'd collar gambler after gambler and tell each of them, "If you spent more time with God and stopped your gambling, your burden would be lightened."

Apparently a lot of sinners agreed with me. During my two-day revival in Las Vegas, more than a hundred people, many of them compulsive gamblers, gave their hearts to Christ and began the wonderful journey toward a new life.

Of all the places I've preached, Vietnam was the most inspiring. When my plane touched down in Saigon, I was met by a colonel. On the ride to the hotel, he warned me, "If you hear a thud against the car—jump! It's probably a hand grenade." I'm not ashamed to admit he scared me. As we drove along, the car hit a bump and I leaped out. I thought

I'd heard a thud. The colonel came over and laughed. "Relax, Reverend, that was only a false alarm."

I was assigned two security officers and by helicopter and jeep I was transported all over the war zone.

Believe me, I didn't meet a single athiest anywhere in Vietnam.

And the closer to battle you got, the less denominationalism there was. When I preached to the First Cavalry Division, Catholic, Lutheran, Methodist, Episcopalian and Jewish chaplains were on the platform with me.

Sometimes I spoke to groups of only three or four men, hovering, deathly afraid, in a foxhole. I shook hands with them and talked about the Lord. I didn't have any trouble winning converts.

One night I slept in a foxhole myself. I was awakened early in the morning by something nudging me. I gingerly shook one of the security officers and whispered there was something crawling around. He got his flashlight out and spotted a rat. "Good thing it wasn't Charlie," he said. When he explained that "Charlie" was GI for Viet Cong, I said, "Send more rats, send more rats."

I found many unsung heroes in Vietnam. I met a married nurse in the Third Field Hospital in Saigon whose husband had retired from the Army and was back in the States. I asked this most dedicated lady, "What motivated you to stay over here, thousands of miles from your husband, to help men you don't even know?" With tears in her eyes, she answered simply, "My faith in God and love for my country."

I'll never forget the grizzled sergeant who had the thankless job of working in our Saigon morgue, tagging and identifying the bodies of our casualties. He was old enough to retire, but had volunteered to stay on because nobody else wanted the job. Walking through that morgue was a grisly experience.

Men so torn up their mothers wouldn't know them. Men without faces, arms, legs, heads. One day the sergeant learned that his son had been killed in action at Da Nang. He requested permission to accompany his son's body back to the States. A tracer was sent out to locate the corpse. Eventually, the sergeant discovered he had handled his own son's body a few weeks earlier and hadn't recognized him.

On many occasions while visiting the hospitals, soldiers and marines would ask me to kneel beside their beds and lead them to the Lord. There wasn't any need to convince them of a heaven and a hell. They knew.

I went to visit our fighting men to encourage them. They ended up encouraging me. Everywhere I went, morale was high, and our boys were committed to the idea that America was playing the role of good Samaritan to the Vietnamese people.

I came home and told my audiences that I felt America was making a tremendous witness for God in Vietnam. The South Vietnamese know that the Communists promise and don't produce, but that the United States promises and produces. Any Christian is anti-war, but being a follower of God doesn't make you a fool.

In reaching out from Bourbon Street, I intend, in the future, to establish branches of my ministry in Greenwich Village, New York, Las Vegas and the Sunset Strip. I also intend to start a soul-winning clinic in New Orleans, a giant hotel where the troubled may come and stay for as long as they like while they search for God. Most of all, I am going to continue preaching the word of the Lord. Each year the revivals and Crusades grow larger and more souls are saved. I'm going to carry the message of the Lord into every major American city until Christ comes into the hearts of millions of people.

Wherever I am in the world, all roads, finally, lead back to

Bourbon Street. There my sin-soaked parishioners wait, drowning in the devil's Disneyland. Because of my work on Bourbon Street, newspaper reporters have called me the "20th Century's Most Unusual Preacher" and "A Man on Fire for God." Those are great compliments, and I will continue to do my utmost to live up to them.

Every day of my life brings new adventure and new insights into the magnificent ways in which Jesus serves His followers. Spiritual and practical experience combine to prove again and again to me the truth of Isaiah 25:1: "O Lord, thou art my God; I will exalt thee, I will praise thy name; for thou hast done wonderful things."

The most dramatic demonstration of that Bible verse occurred in my life one night on the long drive across the twenty-three-mile Lake Pontchartrain Bridge that leads into New Orleans. I had preached that evening and I was exhausted. I was anxious to get home. Midway across the bridge, my headlights picked out the figure of a man jumping up and down, waving his shirt at me. I was going to pass him by. Half-clothed, he looked like a maniac. He's on drugs, I thought, he's going to kill me. He's an escaped patient from the nearby state mental hospital.

The man, standing in the center of the lane, made it impossible for me to drive on. I slammed my foot down hard on the brake.

"Stop, stop, stop," he yelled.

I got out of the car. The man was wild-eyed and wringing wet with perspiration. I shook him hard, and said, "I've stopped, I've stopped. What do you want?" He was too emotionally distraught to speak. Another man came up and said, "Thank him, thank him."

"For what?" I asked.

"A tugboat broke loose and knocked a span out of the bridge and a Greyhound bus is in the lake with six dead."

I hugged that man and fell to my knees and said a prayer.

When I got home, I told Joyce, "Thank God that man had compassion and concern. Thank God he cared. If not, I'd be at the bottom of the lake."

And that's what God is doing. He is standing on the bridge shouting to sinners throughout the world, "Stop, stop, stop, or you perish without Jesus."